Secrets from the Cradle to College Admission
at MIT and the Ivy League

A Parent-Student Guide for
Life Successes in the New Millennium

Earl Ernest Guile

Writers Club Press
San Jose New York Lincoln Shanghai

Secrets from the Cradle to College Admission at MIT and the Ivy League
A Parent-Student Guide for Life Successes in the New Millennium

Published by Writers Club Press
an imprint of iUniverse.com, Inc.

For information address:
iUniverse.com, Inc.
620 North 48th Street
Suite 201
Lincoln, NE 68504-3467
www.iuniverse.com

ISBN:0-595-08969-0

Printed in the United States of America

This book is dedicated to my parents Mr. Earl E. Guile Sr. and Mrs. Evelyn Guile

Contents

Strategies for Excellence

The College Application Process

Preface

The tremendous efforts of my two sons are the basis and the original inspiration for this book. Our focus in this exposition is on Mark, the oldest, because he blazed the academic trail for our family. As we reach the new millennium, the competition worldwide for selective colleges is getting keener each year. This book is intended to be an inspiration to students struggling against tremendous odds for success in life. It is an approach and a philosophy of excellence. Most books of this genre are written from the college admission officer or college counselor's perspective. This book is no guarantee of success. It is merely intended to be a roadmap, from a parent's perspective, on the long-term strategies and actions necessary for students to position themselves for that coveted acceptance by MIT, the Ivy League, other selective colleges in the USA, and universities worldwide. It must be stressed that the parental efforts discussed in this book reflect the true teamwork of both parents. We truly complemented one another in our efforts. Along with the efforts of Mark are the efforts of his younger brother Geoffrey. He has continued the commitment to excellence that his older brother has shown.

This book goes out with the optimism that it will provide parents and students with clear ideas and strategies to reach the stars in colleges, universities and in life.

The following is a speech which was also an inspiration for this book. It was delivered to a group of international honor students. The ideas in the speech became the core ideas for this book.

Worthy of Honor

Earl Ernest Guile

Speech delivered on May 20, 1997 at the National Junior Honor Society Induction Ceremony at the American International School—Riyadh Copyright © 1997 Earl Ernest Guile

Supt. Davis, Mr. Liebzeit, distinguished teachers and administrators, honored students and parents, ladies and gentlemen. It is indeed a pleasure to address you this evening for one of your most solemn occasions, and the night that students receive the highest honor the school can bestow for achievement and promise, induction into the National Junior Honor Society.

You are being honored tonight for scholarship, leadership, service and character. Taken collectively, these ideals constitute the traits of the students we would like to cultivate for the rigors of the 21st century. You are destined to provide needed leadership in this new century and millennium. Your scholarship can open doors but only your character can keep them open. That character will lead you toward service for humankind. Heraclitus, the Greek philosopher, said, *"A man's character is his guardian identity."*

The qualities you are being honored for tonight are important to the world of the 21st century. Individuals who are exemplary in the pursuit of knowledge and in their dedication to service for humankind are critical to the survival of civilization. You have a duty to continue to cultivate and strengthen those qualities in the future. The world needs you. Your future actions shall determine if you are worthy of this honor.

Honorees, what can you do now to stay on course and reach your objectives in life while benefiting the community around you? I will take the liberty to offer a few specific and practical suggestions to you for your immediate future. Many of these are very difficult; you may think I am expecting too much, but these are also your duties because the world needs you. The world expects greatness from you.

1.) Dream dreams and let your imagination soar. Set written goals. A study of Yale University graduates from the 1950s revealed that only 3% of the graduating class developed written goals. When studied years later, that same 3% were very successful in their careers. They continued to write down their goals, and most strikingly, their net worth was greater than the other 97% combined. What lessons can we draw from this story? Written goals take on a power of their own. The Chinese have a proverb which states, *"The palest ink is better than the best memory."* Consequently, you should write down your goals while in junior high and work diligently in the coming years to fulfill them. A written down goal, in some way no one understands, tends to attract every ingredient it needs to realize it. Benjamin E. Mays, the former president of Morehouse College said, *"It must be borne in mind that the tragedy of life doesn't lie in not reaching your goal. The tragedy lies in having no goal to reach. It isn't a calamity to die with dreams unfulfilled , but it is a calamity not to dream…not failure, but low aim is sin."*

2.) Firmly grasp and hold on to your value system in a changing world. Your family has provided you with a set of values and ethics. Keep them for the 21st century; they will serve you well and keep you straight along the tortuous path of a complex world. The Wall Street scandals of 1980s indicated that superior education was not sufficient for success. Education without ethics is empty. Religion and spirituality are very important.

3.) Take calculated risks. Dr. James Bryant Conant, the former president of Harvard University, kept a plastic turtle on his desk with the inscription, *"Behold the turtle! It only makes progress when it sticks its neck out.*" Learn new skills and try new hobbies. Try new sports or a new musical instrument. Find your hidden talents. Change your metaphors.

4.) Develop and amplify your basic academic skills. Read extensively and widely. Read a minimum of one book per week. Intensify your communication skills. Learning how to speak and write are perhaps the most important skills you can have in any career. Francis Bacon, the British philosopher, said, *"Reading makes a full man, speaking a ready man, and writing an exact man."* Incidentally, Mr. Bacon could use a lesson in today's politically correct language.

5.) Get ready for change in the next century. The 20th century has been characterized by incredible changes including armed conflict; pestilence; famine; population increases; environmental change; medical advances; and scientific technological, informational revolutions. The 21st century promises to be even more astonishing in its expectations. You have a duty to prepare here, you have a duty to prepare in high school, and you have a duty to prepare in university for the great frontier of the next millennium.

6.) Sketch your future education strategy now. A good education is invaluable for your future career and livelihood. Furthermore, the effects of an education include having a greater appreciation of the subtleties of life. My father, Mr. Earl E. Guile Sr., said to me long ago, *"Education is something no one can ever take away from you."* It's not too early to begin thinking about college, university, and graduate school. Learn about admission requirements and procedures for your favorite colleges. Write to colleges early and find out how they expect you to prepare for their demanding work. Send out for catalogs and study them.

7.) Determine your strengths. John Dickey, the former President of Dartmouth, said " *The first requirement of being genuinely well educated is to have the capacity of being useful."* Develop ways to be useful and identify yourself as such. Focus on developing academic strengths and extracurricular strengths. Tiger Woods has found a way to be useful, and it certainly goes far beyond playing golf. At a young age, he seems committed and focused on inspiring others, a useful function, indeed. I understand that he has promised his parents to finish Stanford.

8.) Follow a challenging curriculum. Take tough courses and stretch yourself, because you sharpen your study and thinking skills and develop stamina. Don't run **a**way from a challenge in order to merely get high grades. You will perform well, because your standards are already very high.

9.) Learn test-taking skills. Unfortunately, tests are a fact of life and are important. Start early, taking tests such as the SAT-I for college. In the USA, over 50,000 7th graders take the SAT-I five years early to qualify for talented and gifted programs at Northwestern and Johns Hopkins Universities.

10.) Excellence is worth the cost. Pursue several activities and devote several years to them. Learn to juggle many bowling pins. Join school clubs. Get involved or develop your own community-service projects. There are generally four spiritual qualities in those who excel: 1. having a willingness to compete with yourself as well as with others; 2. having a positive outlook on life with less tendency than others to use drugs and alcohol; 3. having a good organization in the use of time and study habits; and 4. having a concern for others, which often earns you the role of leader.

11.) Market yourself. Don't be afraid to present yourself in glowing yet accurate terms. People who need to know you, such as admission officers for boarding schools and colleges, should get this information. Seek interviews and prepare for them.

12.) Respect others in a multicultural world. Forming friendships across cultures is the essence of the world of the 21st century. What you have learned at this school, from people who look different from you and who come from foreign countries, prepares you for spreading the attitudes of tolerance and empathy in your future. Fight injustice and intolerance when you see it. You, as the leaders of the generation that will bridge the second and third millennium, must also build bridges across cultures and peoples.

You are fortunate to attend the American International School. This is truly one of the great schools of the world. You should appreciate your teachers for their excellent teaching.

Parents are also being honored here tonight. Families are extremely important. In your most formative years, the contributions your parents have made are incalculable toward reaching this important milestone in your career. You should keep a deep sense of appreciation for their sacrifices on your behalf. Your parents have cried for you, they have worried about you, they have toiled for you, they dream for you, they have high hopes for you, they have gone to the wall for you. Never, never, never forget what your parents have done for you.

When I think about the struggles of your parents and forebears and about the hardships that lie ahead in the next century, I am reminded of the words of Thomas Carlyle, the British historian, who said:

"Life is not a May-game, but a battle and a march, a warfare with principalities and powers. No idle promenade through fragrant orange groves and green flowery spaces waited on by the choral muses and rosy hours; it is a stern pilgrimage through the rough burning sandy solitudes, through regions of thick-ribbed ice."

Your parents will be proud of you when you follow the ideals of Harriet du Autremont. She said:

"No vision and you perish

No ideal, and you're lost;

Your heart must ever cherish

Some faith at any cost

Some hope, some dream to cling to,

Some rainbow in the sky

Some melody to sing to,

Some service that is high."

I would like to close with the words of the southern educator and mentor of Dr. Martin Luther King Jr.: Dr. Benjamin E. Mays. He said,

"To be able to stand the troubles of life, one must have a sense of mission and belief that God sent him or her into the world for a purpose, to do something unique and distinctive; and that if he does not do it, life will be worse off because it was not done."

National Junior Honor Society honorees, this message tonight goes out on the wing of a prayer that it might do immense good. Thank you and good luck.

Acknowledgments

I express my deepest appreciation to Mrs. Ann Davis, Mrs. Jean Cassin, Professor Yemi Mosadomi, and Mrs. Arup Das who read the manuscript and provided valuable feedback and suggestions. I also thank Mark's teachers and educators including Drs. Darryl Russell, John Davis, Barbara Chase and Charles Vest for their contribution to Mark's preparation for life. I thank my sister, Georgia Montgomery, for encouragement. I thank my wife Ann for her critical role as a mother in raising our children, and for valuable contributions to the formulation and editing of the manuscript. I thank my sons Mark and Geoffrey for their splendid dedication to excellence and for their consistent pursuit of worthy goals. I thank my extended family for all that they have done to inspire me to make this effort to explain our story with the hope that it can do some good for others.

Part I

The Educational Mission: Fundamental Ideas and Beliefs

Introduction

"Education, then, beyond all other devices of human origin, is the great equalizer of the conditions of men,—the balance-wheel of the social machinery."

—*Horace Mann*

In late March of 1996 Mark called home excitedly to tell us that he had gotten a very thick envelope from the Massachusetts Institute of Technology(MIT).The letter from Mr. Michael Behnke, the Director of Admissions, read, " Congratulations! You are admitted to MIT! On behalf of the Committee on Admissions, let me welcome you as a member of the Freshman Class entering MIT in September 1996. You, your family and your school have reason to be proud of your achievements." In order to get this prized letter, Mark began a journey many years ago as a small child. He had great assistance and encouragement from us, as parents, other family members, his teachers and friends. The accomplishment required hard work and sustained effort. For that, Mark deserves all the credit. He decided long ago to seek excellence, and fortunately his quest has been successful. This book is about that journey and the ideas and strategies that were employed. The objective is to provide a roadmap for any individual or family who would like to follow some of the ideas that we developed over the past few years. These ideas are not written in stone, they are things that Mark did which promoted his development as an individual and helped him to begin to realize his potential.

Before our two sons were born, I thought about the need to be an activist parent. I thought that anyone born who were provided with optimal nurturing could realize a fantastic potential in life. In order to provide this nurturing, it was necessary to search the world high and low and begin a thorough research of the relevant issues surrounding this concept. I began reading everything about early childhood development—biology, the psychology, and the sociology of this period. If I could find out the key elements of child-rearing based on sound scientific research and parental love and affection, I could implement them with my youngster to his benefit.

Why MIT and the Ivy League?

The reason this book focuses on MIT and the Ivy League is because of the simple reason that MIT, in particular, represents for the 20th century the most challenging scientific educational program on the planet earth. The 21st century will be even more technologically oriented, and preparation for the new century in a premier technological institution like MIT is a worthy and challenging goal. There was no original strategic plan to specifically get into MIT, however, the original idea was "to shoot for the stars" and establish lofty goals. The Ivy League colleges exemplify these academic stars. They represent to most selective educational institutions in the country and are regularly ranked among the top schools in the country academically. By having this lofty goal, the preparation would potentially qualify our son for these most selective and demanding colleges in America. The positive result of the strategic plan was the opportunity to attend a school that could prepare him for the realities of the 21st century. When our son received the letter announcing that he had been accepted to matriculate at MIT beginning in the fall of 1996 he was prepared to take advantage of this rare opportunity. He also received letters of acceptance from 13 other selective colleges. This book will focus on what happen before that letter arrived. Mark began preparing several years earlier for this possibility.

We started preparing Mark before he was born. This centered on striving to make ourselves knowledgeable parents. We learned the biology of development, with particular emphasis on neural development in order to prepare ourselves for the task of teaching an infant, a toddler, and the teenage years through the successive stages of growth and development. This research paid off. We were keenly aware of the problem of over doing things and possibly stretching the child too far. The knowledge of the biology of development kept us within bounds and balance yet kept us challenging and stretching the youngster. Our philosophy can be summarized to the three most important things to do for your child, by the phrase, " stimulate, stimulate, and stimulate." In order to promote the development of the brain and promote the hardwiring of important connections for learning and intelligence, it has been shown that various and diverse forms of stimulation are necessary. We attempted to do this early in Mark's development and throughout his childhood and teenage years. Organizing informal and formal activities was a systematic way to promote stimulation and motivation.

A potent instrument that we used with the children was the activity list. This idea was very simple. On partial days during the school year and full days during summer vacation, activity lists were prepared that outlined things that can be accomplished throughout the day. As soon as the child is old enough, he has to make out his own list that is then approved by us. This strategy helps to develop structure in the way the child approaches things. This is essentially a to-do list which is key to corporate executives or any workers accomplishing success in their job.

The talent of the upcoming generation is very important for the world of the 21st century and the Third Millennium. There are enormous problems in the world today and greater ones ahead in the next century. We need brains and talent to solve these problems. The education of capable and dynamic talent is needed. The cultivation of this potential talent by well-informed parents is important for the future of the world.

Starting Very Early

"Everyone of us has the potential of greatness, waiting to be developed."

—*Anonymous*

Critical Issues List

- *Provide an exhilarating environment*

- *Stimulate, stimulate, stimulate*

- *Promote the joy of learning*

Mark, our first son, was born in Paramaribo, Suriname, on January 10, 1978. We, as a family, displayed nomadic tendencies by venturing abroad to live and seek the marrow of life in foreign lands. The first land we chose was a small South American country of 400,000 poly-ethnic people on the northeast corner of the continent, which was over 85 % covered by Amazonian rain forest. Mark was born with the help of several midwives, under rather primitive conditions in this tropical land. During the delivery, which took over 10 hours, I spent the day in the delivery room helping coach Mark's mother while reading the book, *Future Shock* by Alvin Toffler. The experience of seeing a new life come into the world was extraordinary and astonishing. We knew as parents that we would have to make a special effort to give this newborn the opportunity to succeed and possibly excel in life. Everything we read emphasized the importance of providing a stimulating environment for children. We took this idea as our theme throughout Mark's childhood. From the day he was born, we played enormously with Mark. Mark was very good natured and was ready for games at any time. We tended to make our games mentally challenging. During his first two years of life we lived in Paramaribo, Suriname. My work hours for the Ministry of Health freed me up in the early afternoon. Upon returning home I'd spend a major block of time with Mark. Words and numbers were central to our interactions. I began calling out numbers when he first came home as an infant from the hospital. Reading children's books to him followed closely. Irrespective of whether I thought he understood, I read incessantly. I intuitively believed that he understood more than we adults gave him credit for.

The research evidence has subsequently revealed that children begin understanding language in the womb. Reading was indeed a pleasure for me, and I could always pickup the beam in Mark's eyes as the words sang forth. These words made him a stimulated baby, in addition to being a happy baby. As he grew older we became more sophisticated in our approach. We acquired a 16-kilobyte Interact computer that utilized audiotape for data input. Although primitive by today's standards, this computer technology became an integral part of Mark's perspective and outlook. He learned his basic mathematical computational skills with the game called Touchdown. As the players advance across the field, he had to calculate the yardage in his head. If he got a certain number correct, he would get a touchdown. This was the visual reward on the screen for his efforts. This made math fun and let him increase his confidence about the subject. We built on this with other math games. We later expanded to word games. Today's games are far more developed and visually appealing and, certainly, any parent should make computers with the best of today's educational materials available for their children.

A favorite trick we employed was to use the refrigerator as a huge household billboard. On this billboard we placed magnetic letters of immense quantity all over the surface. Words, words, words would form and disappear. We always played question-and-answer games regarding words and numbers until Mark took great pride in getting things correct consistently. His esteem was rising rapidly as he progressed from strength to strength. The words on the refrigerator began to become more complex. We kept buying more magnetic letters to keep pace with his rapidly expanding world of words.

By the time we returned to the U.S. to live, Mark was a two-year-old and his younger brother Geoffrey was a one-year-old. We began a systematic exposure of our sons to library books. Our routine was sacred. We made weekly trips to the local library in Beaverton, Oregon. We provided free browsing time for them and gave them a chance to pick out the books that they had the slightest interest in. As parents, we threw in a few books that we thought were interesting and at checkout time we had no less than 20 books on each trip. These books provided reading and discussions during the upcoming week.

Every night before bedtime, we would pull out a book and curl up on the bed and read out loud to Mark. The books were left in a conspicuous place so that any time he wanted to read a book, he could pick up the book and enjoy it at his own leisure. We deliberately attempted to have the books compete with television. We did this by keeping the books in a place close by and keeping the TV off as much as possible.

Overnight, reading became a natural habit for Mark. He easily sailed through those books in a week's time and we were required to increase the number, just to keep pace. It was astonishing to us to see so much interest on his part. He became a voracious reader and listener. It reached a point where we could not put our children to bed unless someone read to them. It was the law, their law. They demanded it. We did not realize it but they were steadily increasing their neuronal linkages through this process and those new nervous linkages were becoming hardwired in their brains.

We focused on acquiring educational-oriented toys. These, we found to further stimulate their thinking and brain development. Most importantly, the toys were a source of fun and enjoyment. The joy of childhood is something we, as parents, never lost sight of, and we found no contradiction between joy and the serious pursuit of knowledge. For example, we stayed away from guns as a toy modality. Over time, we clearly saw that our children were having as much fun as other children who focused on guns. We were particularly attracted to puzzles and problem-solving type toys.

These toys always challenged Mark and, to our surprise, he solved many of the puzzles we bought for him. Of course, some were too difficult and remained unsolved but we worked with him on some of these puzzles to minimize the sense of frustration that he might experience.

Another type of toy we focused on were construction sets. From the myriad of construction sets, Mark could build a universe of things. He was limited only by his imagination. We found this type of toy to be particularly good because true creativity and innovation could manifest itself. The joy and sense of accomplishment he experienced upon completion of a big construction project were boundless. We firmly believe that the emotions the child experienced after building a large airplane, a large ship, or building a city are special feelings that he will seek to duplicate when he gets older.

Later, we found him willing to take on big projects at a relatively young age (more later in the section on Boy Scouts).

The importance of the nervous system's development is exemplified by over 50,000 of a human being's 100,000 genes being devoted to the nervous system construction. During the crucial early development of the brain, there are windows of opportunity that parents and guardians must take advantage of in order to optimize developmental prospects of their children. For example, the syntax-acquiring window may close as early as five years of age. The early wiring of the brain and the early growth spurts suggest that language acquisition begins very early and should be stimulated by parents. Exposure to new words through reading and talking are critical. The baby that is talked to the most advances the most rapidly in language skills.

Modern neurological science with rigorous scientific evidence suggests that the first three-years-of-life is a crucial period in the development of the child's brain and should be exploited for helping the child to optimize his or her potential. The brain at birth has over 100 billion neurons. A stimulating environment is essential. Research indicates that a paucity of stimulation and children who are not regularly touched and played with develop small brains with less synaptic connections between neurons.

Early Schooling Experiences

"Education is difficult and expensive. But whatever it costs, it's cheaper than ignorance."

—*Anonymous*

Critical Issues List

- *The importance of education*
- *Public vs. private*
- *Preschool*
- *Elementary school*

The importance of education

Why is education important? Simply put, the fruits of life are more likely to be realized when an individual is well educated. Contemplate the opposite, for a moment. If a child was put in a dark room and simply fed an adequate diet everyday, he will not develop properly over the years. The child will be a shell of a person without a personality. On the contrary, someone who receives nurturing affection and love during those years will develop the foundation for a healthy life which would probably continue in the late teens with a formal education. A very high percentage of these people will attend a four-year college and possibly a professional or graduate school.

The more education one has, the more your ability is enhanced of experiencing a high-quality life. There are no guarantees about this. An abused child could miss the positive effects of an expensive education. The corollary also has an element of truth. The person, properly raised by the parents or guardians with nurture and love who misses the opportunity to pursue higher education, could through extensive reading and careful observation gain a self-education. For those who were fortunate to gain a formal higher education, an appreciation of life can be reached on a more subtle plane. A great appreciation of the arts, for example, is evident throughout life. However, the arts alone are not a bellwether test of the enhancement of the quality of life resulting from education. The ability to earn a living is also eminently more feasible with a good education. There are strong statistical correlations between educational levels and income potential. A college-degree holder earns several hundred thousand more dollars than a high-school diploma holder. Moreover, an educated person is generally more aware of ethics and of service to the community. These attributes in citizens are important to any civilized society. Clearly, the benefits of education far outweigh the disadvantages.

I think it is very important that we establish a stronger tradition in families regarding the importance of education. One reason that I feel it's important for Mark to gain the experience in strong academic schools is that this experience has proven itself for many generations in America and other countries. By attending rigorous and demanding institutions at a relatively young age, the die is cast for further education and advancement in life based on dedicated and determined effort. That's because quality education is key to the success of a family and a nation. Hopefully, our descendents will have clear message by the institutions that we have matriculated in that we consider education a serious enterprise deserving of a quest for quality. From this message they will then be compelled to pursue just the same. There should be an inner urge unstoppable in all of the children, grandchildren, great-grandchildren, and so forth, for that intangible called education. Education is one thing that no one can take away from you. Also one should " get as much as you can and as fast as you can."

Private vs. public education

There is an ongoing debate about the merits of public school and the relative merits of private school. There is the philosophy on both sides which explain why one is better than the other. We found that the best thing to do was to operate within our means and do what we thought was most beneficial for the child. Parents and children can make the best of situations that they naturally get into. The selective colleges pick over sixty percent of their students from public schools. This is one statistical indicator which confirms that public schools have strong possibilities for preparing children to achieve at a high level.

Preschool

An Italian physician and educator established a worldwide network of schools which bear her name. The philosophy is grounded in science and has spread throughout the world. Started by Dr. Maria Montessori, the system borrows heavily from Piaget, an early childhood educator from Switzerland. While working in a psychiatric clinic, Montessori developed an interest in educating mentally-retarded children. She developed many innovative ways to educate these formerly hopeless children. She also developed a philosophy of education which centered on the child and his needs. She felt strongly that the child had an intrinsic inborn creative potential, an innate drive to learn, and had fundamental rights to be related to as an individual. This potential could be realized through a well-designed educational system which was child-centered.

After developing her ideas working with retarded children whom she saw spectacular progress, she opened a school called Casa dei Bambini or Children's House. She supplied materials and developed a system for children to use these materials to advance their education. Any parent can learn from this system and apply the basic system in their home. These materials included beads for math, wood carved into the shapes of letters and numbers, and a classroom with child-sized furniture. To everyone's amazement, the children would work for extended periods of time in this environment, in this world with few distractions.

Self-direction was the core philosophy. Dr. Montessori felt that children in the right setting could learn on their own and develop a life-long habit of pursuing education. Her medical background promoted a philosophy that biological and mental growth are linked together. This was a radical idea at the time but has been proven in subsequent research.

She traveled throughout Europe, USA, and India lecturing and promoting her ideas. Eventually, schools based on her ideas have been established on every continent. Also, training programs have been established for teachers worldwide.

Because this system has proven strengths, we enrolled Mark in a Montessori school when he was 4 years old. It proved very beneficial.

Why is early childhood formal schooling important? All of the neurological research indicates that the big window of opportunity lies somewhere between birth and five years of age. This is the age range where here-to-fore minimal, formal education has been developed. We were convinced, based on our research, that the Montessori school would be beneficial for Mark.

In Beaverton, Oregon, there were not many choices for early education. The state did not provide public kindergarten class. However, at our first chance, we enrolled Mark in a Montessori school at four years of age. The Montessori school was well-organized and disciplined in its approach to early education. The essence of the system is to understand the critical stages of development and construct an educational system that takes advantage of those stages of intellectual growth.

For Mark, we noticed an immediate effect of his outlook and perspective as he was introduced to this form of education. First, we noticed his strongly positive attitude toward learning and school in general. We felt this alone would justify the investment in his education at this level. Secondly, we noticed that his sense of responsibility, leadership, and maturity grew by leaps and bounds. Shortly after he started, he was assigned the task of helping the young children in various ways. From these early experiences, Mark volunteered to help those younger than he in various situations. This behavior has carried on to this day and has been essential in developing his empathy.

Because of his reading ability, resulting from the weekly library excursions, he was prepared to devour the story reading program of his teacher, Mrs. Meza. Every day he came home with new books, which were getting progressively more difficult. Mark was clearly excited and happy about learning. He made new friends and the school was the central theme in his life now. As parents, we could see clearly that Mark was heading in the right direction. Our investment in his early childhood formal education was paying off. This experience also set the tone for us for the future; we did not see the financial cost as an obstacle to our children's education. Our philosophy became "excellence was worth the cost". A long-range view demonstrated to us that the expense of high-quality education was well worth the cost. The potential for future achievement was enhanced enormously by education.

One question that parents may sometimes ask is the question of early child education being very expensive. Some schools, around large urban centers, are charging as high as $12,000 per year for preschool. This points up to a very philosophical perspective that we, as parents, have taken regarding our children's education. Within our means, we have tried our best to cover any and all educational expenses pertaining to our children. We considered education an investment in their future, although expensive but well worth it.

Of course, many families have limited resources for the children's education. This philosophy can still be followed but expenditures can be held within the limits of the family's resources. Creative approaches which keep costs down can be utilized. For example, home school is a viable alternative to expensive private preschool. There are many resources available which can assist any parent in establishing a home-schooling environment in the home (see Appendix).

Whether a parent opts to utilize home schooling is not, in my opinion, that important. However, it is important that the atmosphere of a home school be established. The resources and materials associated with home schooling can provide a vitally needed sense of education and stimulate the motivation of a child toward learning. One of the key strengths of home schooling is the self-learning skill the child gains. This is a critical skill that many traditional students do not acquire until they reach college years. While the student attends regular school, a self-learning skill strategy would enhance the performance of the child and promote excellence. The foundation in attitude and discipline established will, in later years, carry through the critical periods of college and postgraduate years of education.

American International School Elementary School

As a family, we developed a lifestyle of migratory work. Fortunately, in my profession, it was not too difficult to make a large-scale move, half the way around the world. We migrated at this time from Beaverton, Oregon, to Riyadh, Saudi Arabia. Although we were world's away from America, we discovered an international culture within the traditional world of the Middle East. It was called the American International School.

When Mark enrolled in the American International School Riyadh for the first grade, he was immediately put in a 21st century environment of numerous cultures. There were over 55 nationalities represented in his school. This was a multi-cultural universe and was the norm for him. This school was founded in the early sixties, to provide for an education to the dependents of Americans living and working in Saudi Arabia. It acquired the reputation for academic excellence and became a magnet for other nationalities who came to work in the region. The children attending this school were mostly those of professionals and senior-level foreign workers and diplomats in the country. The teachers were recruited primarily from the USA and Canada. In the school's strategic plan, the school stressed its diversity and developed a long-term strategy to optimize the advantage of having so many cultures under one roof. There were national day celebrations, international dinners, and a curriculum emphasis on learning about other nations and cultures. The children in the school visited each other's homes, and friendships across international cultures were common and the norm. This multicultural environment helped to forge the mindset of the students towards an international perspective and constituted the environment where Mark developed the basic academic skills required to build his future.

This international school worked out very well for Mark and fully justified the continuation of living in Riyadh so that he could complete his junior high education there. Just as public schools range in quality, private schools also have a range of quality. We were fortunate to have in Riyadh a very good school which challenged the students greatly.

When Mark entered the first grade, this was a momentous occasion for both child and parents. I remember driving out to the school and looking for the area where the first graders gathered. Each section of the first grade had a sign and a place for the line to form for all the students on the list of that class. We found Mark's section and he dutifully stood in line. Several other students came and joined the line and began talking with one another as they waited for the teacher. It was very exciting for me as a parent to see my son beginning his first year of elementary school. The school had a reputation of being a very strong academic school. The teacher finally came and greeted the entire group of parents as well as the children. She then asked the children to follow her. All of the parents watch as the children disappeared into the building and down the hall to their class.

There were mixed feelings among the parents as our children were led away. We didn't want to see them go, yet we felt that time marches on and that it was time for them to get their education. From the first day onwards, Mark came home from school very enthusiastic. He had a beam in his eyes that indicated that he was happy. Mark began his first grade year with a strong foundation learned from his preschool years and the year at a Montessori school in Oregon. He, for example, was a confident and skilled reader. He also had a firm grasp of elementary mathematics. The first few months were a breeze for him and primarily served as a review and reinforcement of the basic materials. The work in the beginning was not too hard for him because he was already prepared for basic reading and writing. Many of the lessons of the first few weeks were a reinforcement of things he already knew. From the earliest time of reports, Mark obtained very strong positive evaluations. Teachers were very enthused about Mark. They liked him because of his eagerness and cooperative nature. He always did the tasks required that were mostly graded at an excellent level. A habit of excellence was forming early.

In his first grade year, under Mrs. Gardner, Mark received very good reports. In the first quarter she said, "Mark is a good, reliable student. His grades reflect consistency of his work." In the second quarter she wrote, "Mark continues to do good work and thoroughly deserves his promotion to the pilot reading group." This latter reference was to the special reading group for students who showed particular promise. He enjoyed this achievement and benefited greatly from that group.

By the third quarter Mark had another report which stated, " another excellent semester, well done, Mark!" Mark finished the year with excellent grades in all of his major courses. When they began reading in earnest, Mark was well prepared and progressed in his ability to read quickly and efficiently.

In the second grade, the same comments and grades continued with his teacher. Mrs. Michaels stated, "Mark is doing well this quarter. He is a conscientious student who strives to do his best." She also stated, "Mark was a fast learner, conscientious student, and his work is very promising. Keep it up."

When he reached the third grade, he was well established now in this new school. We had decided to stay in Riyadh, rather than go back home after two years. Later, Mark had a rather distended stomach, and this had gradually gotten larger over the past couple of years. During this time, we were actively visiting the desert. Mark was climbing rocks, sometimes in very dangerous areas. With his large stomach this hindered his physical abilities. We decided to take him for a medical examination at the hospital at King Saud University. A physical exam by the physician found nothing abnormal. But the radiographic exam of his abdomen revealed a cyst that required an immediate surgical operation. We had a choice of having the surgery in Riyadh or in the United States. After a thorough analysis of the situation we decided to take Mark to Stanford University Medical Center, in California, for the surgery.

This required that Mark leave school for a span of time. Before we left to go to the U.S., I went to the school and talked to the teachers and administrators, and they provided me with Mark's books and assignments that would take place over the next few months. This permitted him to continue school work while going to the United States for surgery. Before Mark's trip in November, his teacher Mrs. Barber said, "Mark has done very well academically this quarter, his work is always completed on time and is exceptionally neat. However, I would like to see him do less talking."

Mark returned to Riyadh approximately a month and a half later, just before Christmas. This permitted him to complete the second quarter in the middle of January. At the end of this quarter, where Mark missed nearly six weeks of school, his teacher wrote, "even with Mark absent this quarter, he did an excellent job academically. He is very conscientious about completing his assignments. I'm happy to see him back and I encourage him to keep up the good work." Although it was very difficult for him, Mark worked hard in California while he was recovering from his surgery. With the help of his grandmother, he completed most of the assignments and had the opportunity to keep contact psychologically with his school. When he returned he continued to have a successful third-grade year, and his teacher in the final report said, "it has been a pleasure having Mark in my class this year. He assumes responsibility well, strives for perfection, and is well-liked by his peers. I wish him all the luck in fourth grade."

Over the elementary years, Mark's attitude toward school and work grew more positive and enthusiastic. This propelled me to venture to a board meeting at the school to determine why this school promoted such a positive outlook in its students. What I found was a revelation. The board meeting was a highly harmonious affair where I saw a strong, cooperative relationship between the board and the school administrators. This engendered an atmosphere of excellence and warmth which in turn fostered an atmosphere of multicultural harmony. This incredible example of harmony in an overseas school differed from the acrimonious bickering found in many schools around America.

From this early experience, I decided to begin an active participation in the parental governing of Mark's school. Through this strategy, I could keep abreast of the current issues and critical concepts that were occurring at the school. I could convey those things directly to Mark. This also gave me the opportunity to take part in discussions and make decisions that would affect the policies and strengthen the quality of the school.

I began by joining the educational policy committee of the Board of Trustees. Through this committee, I learned about the standards the school tried to follow in all areas of the curriculum. I also learned about the personnel of the school and other parents and their debating style in these committee meetings. This provided an invaluable opportunity for me to develop my debating style while expanding my understanding of the issues that made the school function.

In order to firm up my commitment to working with the administration of Mark's school, I decided to run for the Board of Trustees at the end of Mark's third year. I joined the list of candidates and lost by a narrow margin. I was second runner-up. During the year, two board members left which necessitated that the two runner-ups join the board. This began what later became a six-year tenure as a board member of the international school. I personally gained a greater understanding of the school and its resources; this resulted in my bringing many of those benefits of the school to Mark directly. I highly recommend that the parent to become involve with their child's school. If not at the board level, the committee, coach or other level is recommended.

Mark's career as an elementary-school student was now well established, and fortunately he was in a school environment which permitted him to be happy and to grow with the challenge of learning. Later in his education at the elementary level, we decided to challenge him further in some of the basic subjects. We purchased extra math, science, reading, and phonetic work books. During the holidays and summer vacations, we challenged him to do the exercises in these books. We were careful to keep a balance. We certainly did not want him to do only work. Play was considered very important. The chance to socialize and make friends was always deemed important.

By the fourth grade Mark joined a class with Mrs. Karen Krech. She wrote a note in October stating that Mark had a B- in language arts, A+ in spelling, A+ in math, A+ in science, and A in social studies; his overall effort was excellent. For comments, Mark is a strong student in all areas. He needs occasional reminders regarding voice volume , is helpful and has good insights into any topics we discuss. I wrote back to the teacher to thank her for her efforts with Mark and I discussed his continued hard-working potential for improvement in the necessary areas and for her to challenge him a little bit extra. We always made it a policy to communicate with Mark's teachers, both face to face and in writing.

Mark continued with this excellent school work and his grades were mostly A's and B's. The teacher's first report stated that "Mark is a capable student with a breath of knowledge. Proofing assignments will alleviate most of his careless errors." In six grade, teacher Mrs. Joan Clemens was very happy with Mark. She said, "I'm pleased with Mark's work and I agree with his evaluation of himself. He needs to improve his organizational skills to prevent a loss of assignments. He usually finds his work." I wrote back that "Mark is a serious and disciplined student and that he can always improve."

She later wrote that "Mark is doing well in school; however, I'm not sure of always getting his best effort in all areas. He did put a lot of effort into his insect world composition, and I enjoyed reading it." It was during this six-grade year, the first year in junior high, that he qualified for the honor roll which required a GPA of 3.7 out of 4. Letters came home from the school that spoke of the encouraging signs of Mark's tremendous growth and progress in school. The Stanford Achievement Test results showed that he had continued to score in the 90th percentile in 11 of the categories that he was tested. It was during this early year in school that we developed a plan to begin taking the SAT exam for college entrance. On the first test there was 320 on the verbal and 310 on the math, for a total score of 630.

During his career at the international school, Mark found students from over 55 countries. We considered this a very important part of his education. The birthday parties Mark was invited to usually had children from various countries. He had a very close friend from Burma, friends from India, Scandinavia, from the Far East, and, of course, many friends from all over America. This dynamic set of friendships have helped to shape Mark's world view and have provided him with insights into various cultural perspectives that would be hard to acquire anywhere else. Mark became very good at making friends. This was the skill I told him that would serve him well in the future. This contributed very much to his happiness as a student. Mark continues to communicate with many of the friends he made at the international school. (More about this in the section on learning from others)

In the beginning Mark devoted about half an hour to 45 minutes to homework in the first grade. He never complained but dutifully he began his work immediately after coming home from school and eating a snack. Over the years, the time gradually grew to approximately 2½ hours. His routine consisted of doing his homework first, then other activities including play. Our focus also was on him to go to bed by 8:30 in the evening during his early years and this gradually increased to 9:30 or 10:00 p.m. by the ninth grade.

Child-Parent Relationships: What Does It Mean To Be A Parent?

"The best legacy parents can leave their children is a sound education."

"When you praise another, you enrich yourself more than you do the other."

"Praise often turns losers into winners."

—Anonymous

Critical Issues List

Parent-Child Interactions

- *Build trust*

- *Show empathy*

- *Listen*

- *Allow free time*

- *Avoid comparing*

- *Right to privacy*

- *Child may have ups and downs*

- *Can backtrack*

- *Make his own choices*

- *Set limits to the behavior*

- *Help your child discover his talents*

- *Establish authority*

- *Develop good communication*

- *Build friendship*

- *Be there for your child*

- *Keep a balance*

- *Help manage peer pressure*

- *Develop emotional intelligence*

Long before actually being a parent I thought carefully about this role in life; this huge responsibility, this unbelievable tax and labor that one volunteered to do. I even wrote about it—I remember writing while riding on a ferry in Hong Kong during the time I lived in that city. There, I wrote incessantly on how I would focus my energies on this opportunity when it presented itself to me.

When parenthood began for me it was a special feeling. It was an undeniable joy to hold someone from a long lineage, heritage, and familiar patrimony. The vital questions were: what must be done now to help this new human being become a good productive citizen and as new parents how can we promote the optimization of the baby's potential?

Dr. Benjamin Spock, the author of the classic child rearing book *"Baby and Child Care,"* said to parents, " Trust yourself. You know more than you think you do…Don't be afraid to kiss your baby when you feel like it." This is the advice that our family followed. Our job as parents was to provide an environment of love, care, and affection along with the constant stimuli to help the personality and mental ability of the child flourish in conditions conducive to robust development.

The minutes, hours, days, months, and years spent with children can become powerful unrelenting stimuli to their self-realization and intrinsic to their ability to cope with the ups and downs attendant to the ebb and flow of life itself. The process of seeing the baby transformed into a competent, contributing adult inspires the parent.

Building trust

Good parenting is the best way to build trust between you and your child. The following are a few tips on key parenting issues. Most parents want their children to be successful in life. It would be a bonus if the children can also be reasonably happy. How can a parent help their child attain these coveted goals? There's no such thing as a perfect parent. Parents are human and they have weaknesses and vulnerabilities like anyone else. We have to be logical parents. Logical parents show empathy to their children. That means parents have to be able to put themselves in the child's shoes, even when there is disagreement. The mix of understanding parental feelings as well as the child's feelings gives an openness that children appreciate.

Learn your role as a parent. *Listen to your child in a non-judgmental way.* When you listen to them talk do not interrupt, and do not try to outwit them when you talk. Stop blaming your child for everything that goes wrong. Express your feelings openly and honestly but don't blame everything on the child. Don't ignore serious problems when they occur. Keep the lines of communications open so you can discuss them frankly. Appreciate the differences between you and your child, and respect your child for his uniqueness.

A child does not have the same work ethic as an adult. Therefore, do not expect him to have the same attitudes about work. If he sits around and dream, this is not necessarily bad. A child needs time to dream about the future, to contemplate faraway lands, and to plan his life ahead.

Dream time can be very valuable in a child's experience. The children some-times show strange behaviors and have strange conversations with their friends but don't be alarmed. There is a function for this behavior. During telephone conversations with their friends, they are clarifying positions and opinions about life with them. Of course, there are times when the child has to do work (as outlined in the chapter on schedules). This also is very important in order to develop discipline. However, parents have to show balance and allow free time and free space. The child needs time to do whatever he wants as well as follows the rules and stays within the con-fines of law.

It is important for parents to avoid comparing their child to another sibling or to another friend of the child. Children are very frustrated by compar-isons, and the message that you send to them is "I believe that you are inferior." Emphasize the uniqueness of your child, rather than how he stacks up against another person. Focus on the problem that you find rather than focusing on the good qualities of another child as an example.

How do you get your child to perform a task or do something that he should do? *Do not nag.* You must first become aware of your constant nag-ging before you can get your child to do something about it. Children get turned off by this and the message you send to them is "trust is not there." Do things to indicate trust with your child. If you can successfully stop the nagging process, your child will consciously do things to please you when he recognizes that you are beginning to trust him. Build on this trust because it will be crucial for future interactions.

Children have a right to privacy. Many parents cannot understand this and they impose themselves on the children as if they have absolute rights over their personal space. We have to change and realize that children need some privacy from the prying eyes of the parents. Show respect of the pri-vacy of the child as you would expect them to show respect for your own privacy. There are of course limitations because if a parent suspects illegal behavior, then privacy may need to be modified. In a conversation where parents need information and if the child does not give information, don't force him to talk.

Children have a right not to reveal the details of conversations they have with others and friends. They don't have to tell you everything. Give your child a chance to be alone when he wants to be. When your child withdraws from the world, this may only be a phase of development. This type of withdrawal may be very important.

Sometimes a child may have ups and downs and can become moody. We have to learn to live with these changes of moods, and we should not worry about a child who have moods sometime. As well, a parent should not dampen enthusiasm when the child is enthusiastic and seems very excited about life and things in general. This could be very significant and is very important to encourage it, recognize it, and praise it. That same enthusiasm should be around for very important projects and tasks. If, for example, you have serious questions about what your child is enthusiastic about, it may be best to wait until the enthusiasm is less before raising your doubts. This is especially true if he is around his friends. It is a very important rule not to criticize your child around his friends because he will feel very bad and may never forgive you for that.

If your child is depressed it is very important to be a listener. If possible, let the child solve the problem on his own. It gives him more self-esteem and more confidence. Back off in the beginning with advice. Sometimes problems will work themselves out without parental involvement. If it is, of course, a serious problem, then you should be willing to provide suggestions and ideas which can help your child through the crisis.

Maturity is a very elusive goal in life and it's very volatile. *The child may show very good maturity one moment, and the next moment he may show much less maturity.* They can backtrack easily. So be prepared to expect that and not be surprised; accept it and be prepared to talk about it. When your child shows limited maturity, don't show anxiety and worry. Be reassuring, show that you have a steady hand in a crisis. This is very reassuring for the child.

Be prepared when children in their teenage years criticize parents. Be prepared to accept the criticism if it is done in a polite way. Set ground rules. With a little maturity, they can guide parents and show their ideas about parental perfection. The parents have to put this all in perspective and show humility and make it clear to the child that they are not perfect. *If your child criticizes you do not become defensive, put it in perspective and move on.*

Don't overdo your role as a parent. *Give your child a chance to make mistakes, to make his own decisions, and to make his own choices.* Modify your role as a parent as the child gets older. Instead of overseeing everything, give your child space and allow him to make decisions. Build trust with the child and when he makes decisions he considers all that it implies, including implementation. There is a universal need among teenagers to feel independent, to feel that they are making their own choices, and to feel self-confident about their abilities. Give your child plenty of opportunities to make decisions. When it is time to make the final decision on a very sensitive topic it is important that you make input, suggestions, and ideas. A parent, however, should let the child make the final decision and be satisfied with it. Our strategy regarding important decisions was for our son Mark to make them. We suggested that we provide some input.

Every parent has to set limits to the behavior of the children. The local rules that the child follows while living in your household hopefully will last for a lifetime. If those limits or rules are not made clear, the child may step beyond the limits. Therefore, it is every parent's duty to make sure the rules for living in the house are explained. It is best to work out goals and limits while sitting down on a one-on-one with the child. Have him agree to the limits, and if the limits are not understood then have discussions that explain them clearly. Once a child understands the limits and the rationale behind them, he would be willing to follow and agree. As your child becomes more mature, rules and limits can be modified to reflect growth and development. Responsibilities should increase and the rules should decrease as the child grows and matures. These limits that you establish should be stable and reassuring, rather than complicated and unstable.

A positive trend toward teenagers is to encourage them to associate with positive peer groups. The parent should put them in these groups, especially when they are young. As the child grows older, he will normally gravitate to those positive peer situations. The child needs to be informed that success depends on his skills and talents and the type of people he associates. The environment also plays an important role. That is why we always tried to get Mark into challenging school environments where the peer group, rather than the teachers, generates more pressure toward excellence.

It is important for you to help your child discover his talents. As adults, we are generally specialized in a particular skill in our professional job. On the other hand, we expect children and teenagers to be good in all the subjects they take in schools and to excel in some sports. They are anything but specialists. We need to systematically expose our children to various activities so that we can discover their talents, in addition to achieving high academics and excellence in sports. Give them many other activities to participate in. You can then learn whether they like it, enjoy it or have a special talent in it.

Encourage your child that it is alright to use trial and error while attempting to discover hidden talents. It is perfectly okay to try something and fail, rather than not to try at all. When your child sees others who are proficient and quick to learn new skills, inform him that people learn at different rates and speeds and there is nothing wrong with that. Achieving at a high-level academically and in sports are not the only priorities in life. There are many other things that your child can discover that may reveal a strong capability and high level of talent.

How should a parent deal with crisis with a child? A parent should show unconditional positive regard and provide non-judgmental support.

In a crisis, emotional and unconditional support is more important than teaching a lesson about the event that occurred. Understand that experiencing some crises from time to time is a normal part of life and that the child must be able to deal with them. A parent should not get overly upset when a crisis occurs. Instead, they should be an ocean of stability in the face of the unremitting chaos. The most dangerous thing at this time is to get angry. Anger can shut off all channels of communication with your child, and at this moment communication is vital to finding a solution and resolving the crisis. As much as possible, listen to your child and have him solve the crisis with your support. This will give him confidence to face future crises in the years ahead. First, focus on the feelings of the child regarding the situation, then focus on solving the problem. Do not try to give instructions on some general principle in the beginning. At this time of crisis, this can have the opposite of the desired effect. Be there for your child and give him all your attention. Take off time from work if necessary. Show your sincere commitment to the crisis. This will go a long way toward building a strong bond between you and your child. This in effect, turns a negative situation to a positive one, a bad thing to a good thing. Your child will never forget the support that you show. They will grow to trust you more and respect you for your support for his well-being.

Be relentlessly positive toward your child. This becomes a self-fulfilling prophecy. Find something to praise him about. Reward him with verbal awards and respect. Remember, you cannot praise your child too often. A parent should praise when a child deserves praise, and not when he does not deserve praise.

Set high expectations of behavior for your child and chances are he will achieve high expectations. Don't present unrealistic expectations bordering on the impossible. Have expectations within the realm of reality and something the child can buy into and positively seek. Have fun with your child and do things with him that build a parent-child bond. Enjoy activities together and do them on a regular basis. Take camping trips and plan them a few weeks in advance.

Discipline

The question of disciplining your children is a difficult one for any parent. There are several principles that should be followed. *Parents have to establish authority over the children but they should do it in a way which is compatible with the child's psychological well-being.* Make a determination of when a punishment is required and only punish when punishment is really necessary. When punishment becomes the norm and the routine, it loses its effectiveness. It should be a relatively rare event. Also, avoid overly harsh punishments. If your child plays with the computer games when he should not, cancel the computer games for one day. If you cancel for two weeks it may be a little bit harsh for the infraction. Delaying the punishment can be a problem. Specify what the child did wrong and clearly link it to the penalty.

Follow through with promised punishments. If punishment is promised and is not delivered, the child will lose confidence in your word and authority. Be flexible, and in some cases, if the infraction falls within the confines of normal childhood behavior, be forgiving of it if it's not of major consequence. Do not only punish for minor problems, let the punishment fit the problem. Keep eye contact with your child when you are discussing the problem.

Rather than punish the child for bad behavior, it is probably more productive to reward a child when he does something right or good, especially a verbal reward. You could consider giving a nonverbal reward if the behavior is so good that it needs additional consideration. This strengthens the good behavioral pattern.

Develop good communication

As parents, we always stressed keeping lines of communications open with the children over the years. This began very early through continuous conversations and dialogue. I always formulated numerous questions in which I asked Mark for answers when we were in situations where we had time together. This was particularly fruitful in the car. When he was very young I posed factual questions for his response; as he grew older I'd develop conceptual questions which had him think more deeply about the answers. The factual ones were in the "what" category and the conceptual ones were in the "why" category. Examples of such questions include, "What is the capital of Ecuador?" and "Why is the universe expanding?"

In establishing these channels of communication, parents must listen carefully to what children say. The condition of unconditional positive regard is also essential. When communication becomes difficult, for example, when solving problems, the child always understands that your love is paramount. This is most important in keeping communication channels between parent and child wide open.

We always set aside time to talk each day. Meals were times in which we all gathered together to sit and eat. We made a rule in our family that this was the one time each day that we would all be together at least once. This was not a time to solve problems or deal with difficult issues. It was a time to reflect on today's event and talk about situations and light-hearted things encountered. Through building this base of communication over the years, by the time Mark completed elementary and junior-high school the foundation was established for long-term communication.

When the internet evolved with e-mail, we continued in our pattern of communication via the Internet. Over the difficult years of Mark going to boarding school and beginning of college, we were able to maintain strong, almost daily, communication on important events in his life. It has provided a platform for us to continuously write words of encouragement and offer praise. He felt free to either call by telephone or write by e-mail to ask questions and to convey his feeling on various matters. Of course, as he grew older and his academic schedule grew more demanding, there was less time for regular communication. We, therefore, would continuously send messages of encouragement on positive optimism routinely anyway. We felt that this was important to keep his focus for grueling late-night work and unbelievably high volumes of work.

Build friendship

Building friendship with your child is key to your long-term relationship. Although you are always a parent and they are always the child, friendship and camaraderie are helpful to break the ice and keep it broken. When there's trouble, people go to friends for help. When your children come to you for help in times of trouble and difficulty, this indicates their feeling of friendship toward you. Having a friendship doesn't preclude them from respecting you, and they'll keep the relationship which helps to prevent various problems from developing. It also helps to prevent what has been termed the "generation gap."

Be there for your child

One of the ten best ideas for good parenting should include being there when your children need you. In the formative years, children need the verbal and physical presence of the parents. One cannot emphasize the verbal communication too much. Parent talk, just like self-talk, is crucial to the future image the child has of him/herself. This is the great engine that builds self-esteem. If that roar is negative and demeaning, the ideas stick to resurface again. The dialogue should be positive, uplifting, challenging, praising, stimulating, enriching, motivating, counseling, activating.

Parents can discuss cultural values, intellectual ideas and spiritual issues. The parents should be there physically to set the example. Children will model themselves after their parents. If the parents are absent, the modeling will falter. Parents speak more by their actions than their words. Parents should be able to manage crises during the growing up period.

Keep a balance

In raising a child, it is very significant not to become too fanatical about any one particular thing for your child. Don't go overboard with sports, don't go over board with academics—just keep a balance. Sometimes, it is very difficult to know when you cross over the line with a given activity. A rule of thumb that we found useful was to make everything fun. Of course, some hard work was not taken as fun in the beginning. Point out those elements which could be interpreted as fun. If the mind-set of the child was to interpret things as fun the child would be much more inclined to follow through, develop the habit, and persist with the given activity.

If you find that the activity causes too much stress and creates problems it is very critical to back off and moderate the activity. An activity should not become a stress-provoking nightmare. The failure to back off will turn the child against the activity in question. The sense of proportion in pursuing excellence will help your child learn limits and how to work within these limitations. It is still very important in academic subjects as well as developing proficient skills in other activities.

A friend of mine decided that he wanted to be a good father for his son. He took him to several teachers in martial arts at the age of three years. His son became proficient in several martial arts styles, acquiring a black belt before the age of seven. By the age of nine, the father had an activity schedule mapped out, nearly six months in advance for his son. After school, the child regularly trained and studied various sports with trainers until 11 or12 at night. Those sports included gymnastics, cross-country running, competitive swimming, and ballet. The child eventually ran a marathon at the age of 8 years, and the father had plans for him to swim the English Channel and to later star in martial arts movies. I thought this father's approach was more than I would recommend. This may work only if the child is extraordinarily resilient. Caution was our philosophy.

Children do need the opportunity to grow up and have free time to waste. This overload approach is uncalled for and beyond the scope of reason. Moreover, this can lead to burn out of the child.

All parents should keep the necessity of balance in mind while raising children. This balance, of work and play, academic and non-academic, humor and seriousness, and time on task and free time, is very important in a child's development. We tried to think about this issue with Mark and we pulled back when we thought things were getting out of balance.

Learning from others and managing peer pressure

The best way to manage peer pressure is to constantly strive to put your child in peer situations where the pressure is positive. It is amazing how positive peer pressure can be such a benefit to the child and his motivation. It is quite clear that children respond more to peer pressure than to pressure from parents and teachers.

When your child gets into situations where the pressure is negative, there is a specific strategy to minimize the effect. Children should learn how to handle peer pressure on their own. They have to learn to stand up to the pressure. When they are successful in managing those situations, they will develop more self-confidence. When your child complains about situations with their peers, listen carefully to their feelings and point of view. Show empathy and don't be judgmental. If a problem arises with your child in front of their friends in your presence, do not confront him at that time. Wait until you are home with him and then discuss the matter to get his view. Afterward, you should point out the positive and negative aspects and see whether the child understands your point of view.

When your child is hurt from the teasing and criticism by peers, it is very important for you to help build his self-esteem. Always acknowledge the feelings first. Use phrases such as "I know how you feel when you are angry" and " I was there once and, it is pretty tough." Make your child feel better, by giving praise for standing by principles and standing up to the pressures in life. Children always benefit from giving them praise, no matter how small.

Ideally send your child to a school where all the children are highly motivated for activities and academics. This beehive mentality will transfer to your child. This is one more reason why we have to build institutional success where the majority of the children are on the positive achievement track. The atmosphere will do a better job of keeping everybody on this course of action. Students can do a far better job than a teacher or administrator in influencing other students for the good.

Develop emotional intelligence. The concept was developed in book-length form by Daniel Goleman. His thesis is to give equal time in education to the development of emotions. Indeed, he says that emotional development is key to success in life. His book, titled *Emotional Intelligence*, provides valuable information for any parent on parenting. There is a significant amount of research that supports this hypothesis. A report from the National Center for Clinical Infant Programs titled "Head Start: The Emotional Foundations of School Readiness," in 1992, has focused on several areas as very important for the child. It states that precocious talents in reading and factual knowledge are less a predictor of success than emotional and behavioral skills. These include: the ability to follow directions, waiting ability, expressing needs, self-control of behavior. The seven major areas of competence stressed by Goleman are:

"1.   Confidence

Self-efficacy and a sense of control over one's destiny. The ability to expect success and find help when needed.

2.   Curiosity

Wondering about the world around you is a positive feeling.

3.   Intentionally

Linked to confidence about this trait reflect the sense of ability to affect things and the motivation to act.

4.   Self-control

This is the ability of control behavior and fine tune interaction with others.

5.   Relatedness

The ability to show empathy and to be understood.

6.   Capacity to communicate

The ability to transmit and receive ideas, thoughts, and feelings with peers and non peers.

7.   Cooperativeness

This is essentially the ability to work and play with others effectively."

Goal Setting

"If you're serious about success, you'll make goal setting your first love and self-mastery your second."

—*Anonymous*

Critical Issues List

- *Setting long-term goals*
- *Short-term goals or activity list*
- *Scheduling and planning*

Goal-setting philosophy

Conceptually, establishing the habit of setting goals is possibly the most powerful habit a person can develop. Why have goals and why should you write them down? Goals can become the psychological engine that you can use to create a preferred future. It has been demonstrated in military and business that the planning and implementation of goals are very instrumental in determining the survival and success of the enterprise. Organizations establish goals and give themselves deadlines to beat. During the period, the people in an organization mobilized themselves by going into action and periodically evaluating the progress toward reaching their objectives. Individuals should do the same. Young individuals will have many years ahead of goal-setting and actively pursuing them; these years can be filled with the most rewarding activity of their life. Be imaginative when setting goals, do not let the word "impossible" enter your mind as you speculate. Make sure that these goals are things that you really want and are prepared to work hard to accomplish them.

The same principles apply to all types of goals that you might set, including educational goals. It is through education that your skill level and knowledge level provide the basic tools to achieve a wide range of goals. When you pursue educational goals at a young age, you unleash the power within to accomplish goals in all areas. You can achieve goals professionally, socially, in sports activities, community service, and in personal and leisure areas. You can develop a list of goals in all of the above areas, but we shall focus primarily on developing educational goals.

In your spare time, you should sit down and make a list of all the educational goals that you would like to achieve. Next to that list, put down the number of years it would take you to achieve these goals. Make estimates and don't worry about precision. When making these goals, aim high. Deliberately make the goals that you might even have doubts about completing. Next, put a time estimate for accomplishing the goals. Make a brief statement about why you would like to achieve these goals. Take a look at this list and then set it aside for 24 hours. Look over the list again and either add additional goals or remove goals that you would not be able to attain presently. Afterwards, write the steps that it will take to fulfill each goal and put a time-line estimate for each step.

These goals could include things such as completing the bachelor's degree, a master's degree, and a Ph.D. degree for a particular field. Also, you could include the goal of attending a certain school, especially highly selective universities. They may seem out of reach now, but by establishing a highly selective university as a goal, you create a compelling desire in your mind to go there and you can begin to work hard to fulfill the requirements that such a school will require.

Critical Issues List

The following are some sample questions that you can use for establishing your educational goals:

- Do you want to go to MIT, Harvard or Princeton?

- Do you want to graduate first in your class at high school?

- Do you want to qualify for a talented and gifted program?

- Do you want to get a MBA at Stanford?

- Do you want to go to medical school at Johns Hopkins or go for a law degree at Yale?

Mark used to talk about the colleges he wanted to attend. He wrote down goals regarding those colleges. They became ingrained in his thinking. It was no accident that he ended up going to MIT because he certainly thought about it many years before. We even purchased T-shirts with the name of the college in order to stimulate his long-term thinking.

After you have develop your list of goals, including long- and short-term ones, it is important to write down the number of years you think it might take to reach that goal. Then next to each goal, write a paragraph describing the "what" and the "how" of obtaining that goal. Be very specific about the daily tasks you need to begin to work on right away, in order to make that goal attainable.

Then take these goals and have them printed on the computer on one page, if possible. This paper should then be placed in your room where you can see them on a daily basis. You'll then be constantly reminded of the goals and they will become an ingrained part of your thinking. Every year, you should evaluate your progress toward accomplishing these goals, whether you are doing the things that are needed in order to reach your objective. It is important to quantify your progress.

Mark's goals in his own words

These are a list of Mark's goals that he brainstormed while in the 7th grade. They are written in his own words. Some of the goals he reached and others have not been reached yet.

Goals of 1991 by Mark Guile

Thursday May 23 1991

Format: 1. Goal listed
           A. Timeline
           B. Strategy

Personal development goals

1. Learn martial arts
           A. Two years
           B. Take lessons

2. Be become a better swimmer
           A. In One-year
           B. Swim harder

3. Bike 100 miles
           A. Map out a route to take
           B. One month

4. Get straight A's
           A. Zero minutes

5. Do well in school

6. Become an eagle scout
           A. One half years
           B. Complete all the requirements

7. *Go on a long trek, trail*
> A. *Two years*

8. *Learn to drive*
> A. *Three years*

9. *Read more*
> A. *0 minutes*
> B. *Start reading*

10. *Learn programming*
> A. *Five months*
> B. *Read about programming more*

11. *Type faster*
> A. *Two months*
> B. *Start practice*

12. *Get into 4 Kingdom wide events swimming*
> B. *Swim harder*

13. *Do experiments with the laser*
> A. *Four years*
> B .*Study parts of laser*

14. *Get a better computer*
> A. *Two years*
> B. *Study*

15. *Read War and Peace and Crime and Punishment*
> A. *Two months*
> B. *Start reading*

16. *Finish Encyclopedia Britannica*
> A. *Six months*
> B. *Start reading*

17. *Get better at trumpet*
    A. *Two months*
    B. *Practice hard*

18. *Have a better attitude*
    A. *80 minutes*

19. *Read all the National Geographic magazines*

20. *Get good marks of all my subjects*

21. *Do not get bad marks in my subjects*

22. *Get qualified next year for the kingdom wide and the citywide swim meet*

Career goals

1. *Become a medical person, scientists, or engineer*
    A. *Eight years*
    B. *Study hard during college*

2. *Make a laser or a computer from scratch*
    A. *Eight years*

3. *Learn the laser and computer functions and their parts*

4. *Find a cure to AIDS or cancer*
    A. *Ten years*

5. *Study aids and find weak spot in the virus*

6. *Get better at music*

7. *Get a scholarship*
    A. *Two years*

8. *To become good at certain things*

9. *Make a robot that moves and talks*
>   A. *Two years*
>   B. *Study the way of motion and the parts of already built robots*

10.*Building a model airplane*
>   A. *Ten months*

11. *Study Aerodynamics*

12. *Make ozone in large enough quantities to send up to the atmosphere*
>   A. *Unknown*
>   B. *Study the elements that makeup the ozone and try to construct a stronger version*

13.*Help Ethiopia fight famine*
>   A. *Time unknown*
>   B. *Look at Ethiopia's water table underground*

14. *Build a radio from scratch*
>   A. *1/2 year*
>   B. *Study sound waves*

15. *Make a lot of programs*
>   A. *One year*
>   B. *Learn basic in greater depth*

The Importance of a Value System

"Personality can open doors; only character can keep them open."

—Anonymous

Critical Issues List

Critical questions about maturity and success

- *What are the qualities that will ensure our well-being in the 21st century?*

- *What predicts success?*

- *What is the relationship between test scores and success?*

- *Who are the most effective functioning adults you know?*

Douglas Heath, an educational psychologist researcher, studied 68 Haverford College graduates over a long-term prospective study. One report entitled, *"Academic Predictors of Adult Maturity and Competence,"* established as its objective to find the critical predictors of future success in life. This decades-long research led him to the conclusion that the most important precursor of success was psychological maturity. Most people mistakenly believe that high grades are the best predictors of success but that is not true. Psychological maturity obtained at an early age is the most important factor. There are many things which reflects psychological maturity. Among them is the concept of easily making good friends. The researcher felt that this was so important he felt parents should reward their children for making friends the same way we reward them for making high grades. Consequently, I made it a point to ask Mark about new friendships. If I discovered he made any new ones, I would praise him and express pleasure. Other factors that reflected maturity such as having empathy and respect were also encouraged and promoted. A sense of excellence along with a sense of maturity was considered very important elements for him to incorporate into his character.

Research suggests that the qualities which insure success include having a sense of humor, confidence, energy and enthusiasm, empathy, risk-taking, tolerance, integrity, commitment and devotion, intelligence, adaptability and listening skill.

Other qualities necessary for surviving in the 21st century include caring, adaptability, morality, stress handling, commitment, and skills to survive vocational change.

There is irreversible change taking place in the world today. This is exemplified by the changing role of women. In a survey to determine whether the wife's career is equal to her husband, 40 percent said "yes" in 1969 while 81 percent said "yes" in 1973. When asked the question, "Do I expect my husband to share equally at home," 17 percent said "yes" for women in 1969, while 43 percent said "yes" in 1973.

There are also changes in the vocational world. Computers are very important in the workplace today. Surplus personnel are another problem in many fields. During the 1980's the American Bar Association esti-mated that there were 96,000 surplus lawyers. Over 45 percent of lawyers are bored with their work. Dental schools were closing and there were over 10-percent surplus physicians, 12-percent surplus surgeons, 45-per-cent surplus obstetrics and gynecology physicians, and a 20-percent shortage of psychiatrists. Conditions have changed again in the 1990's. Managed care has reduced the income of physicians and many people are walking away from the profession. It is clear that the students of today most be prepared for even greater changes in the professions of the 21st century. Education will be key to coping with these expected changes.

The half-life of technical information is now only seven years long. There is an early burnout in the pursuit of money, status, and power.

What advice can be given to a young person pursuing a career today? The highest priority in education is to empower the individual for self-education. Ideally, children should find out that they can learn. Boys are generally weaker in languages and girls are generally weaker in science. Parents should monitor the attitude of the children over whether they can do something. Most children learn for extrinsic reasons. But they should be learning for the joy of learning. Interpersonal maturity is very important and should be learned from others. Children who can learn without help and plan and set sub-goals demonstrate self-educational skills.

Educational psychology research suggests that there is a relationship between self-education skills and high grades. Studies to determine the predictability of effective functioning adults have used college students who have been followed through various stages of life. These include professionals, actors, musicians, and civil servants. In order to find out what predicts success, factors such as communications skills, relationship with spouse, sex life, parenting skills, vocational happiness, value system, childhood happiness, and what life was like in this home for several days were evaluated. Were most of the people in the study happy? Yes, 85 percent considered themselves happy. Most consider the '40s the most happy in life and the period where they could erase self-doubt. This was in spite of monetary problems in many cases. The people in the study were remarkably accomplished people; many had written books, created businesses and there was remarkable continuity in personality development. The most destructive behavior among the study group was alcoholism. Of the ones who became alcoholics, five percent of both men and women pulled themselves out of it.

When determining the characteristics of happiness, over 16 characteristics were linked. Interpersonal maturity had a very important link to happiness. A person who is open to new ideas and new experiences is also happy. And those who were better integrated in their lives were happy.

The characteristics that were most strongly associated with happiness in the study group were: caring, honesty, humor, openness, tolerance of people, imagination, dedication, understanding others, respect of others, flexibility, and sensitivity. Other factors that were more important than grades were sense of humor and sensitivity.

Then what predicts success? Grades, for example, predict nothing. The "C" student is just as likely to be an effective manager and an effective person in life as the "A" student. The SAT is no measure of competence in later life. Generally, the higher an aptitude of the SAT the less satisfying were relationships, the less well integrated the person in life, and the less self-confidence they had. It has been said that stripping character and will are more important criteria for accepting people into a profession and grades. Over the last 20 years medicine, for example, has moved from feeling to research centered. The crisis in other professions such as engineering are clearer where many think that the high percent of students have doubts about relationships because of the lack of knowledge of the opposite sex. A study at Harvard revealed that there was no relationship between SAT scores and success. A follow-up was done on dropouts at Harvard and it was found that they scored higher on the SATs and those with psychiatric reasons for dropping out scored much higher.

In a 25-year study of managers at AT&T, those with the highest aptitude tended to be people who were less happy and more maladjusted. This has led to the hypothesis that the higher the aptitude the more the risk. It is possible that children who are more talented are less integrated in life. In many cases, children with higher aptitude had fewer friends and were not sensitive to others. Those who were most academically talented initiated fewer contacts with their peers. Highly talented children who made contacts with their peers generally have more interpersonal maturity.

What are the predictors of success? The SAT-I exam provides no clue to intellectual maturity. The best predictors are extracurricular and self-sustaining activities and hobbies of the child. Are you a loving parent who has firm expectations of the children? Parents have to be good role models for the children. The father and the mother should be actively engaged in the education of the child. The care and concern for the emotional health of the child are very critical to the early years of growth and development. The relationship between parent and child should be based on unconditional positive regard.

In the *Art of Loving*, Eric Frome describes something called the unconditional mother's love which gives the children the feeling that they are loved for who they are. But what predicts whether a daughter will turn out to have a fulfilling motherhood? The best predictor is a parental home that is not tensed with conflict. The parents enjoyed being parents, were openly affectionate, and the children knew that their parents loved them. The mother was usually warm and affectionate, verbally expressive, respected by the father, and the daughters were encouraged to be independent.

However, the most important predictor of an effective functioning adult is psychological maturity at an early age. The child is psychologically mature when he has an understanding of self and is able to put into symbols experiences, perceptions and reflections. This child at this stage has grown out of a self-centered way of looking at things. A psychologically mature person shows empathy for others and is respectful and tolerant of others. This is also called internal coherence, which is demonstrated by relational thinking, values, and integrated mutual concern for others. The psychologically mature child is also more stable, resilient under stress, and his values in life are more positive too. This child also has a system for learning and applying the knowledge learned to new situations. He has the ability to refuse drugs and alcohol in spite of peer pressure.

By the time a child reaches 17 years, he has spent 17,000 hours watching television. Some of the television programs are very professional such as Sesame Street which promote the need for entertainment in children. This predisposes the child to be bored. If you take these many hours out of his house life, there will be less time for reading, cooperative behavior, and hobbies. It is therefore important to reduce TV time and replace that time with those productive activities that can support the development of psychological maturity in your child.

Ethics

Teaching ethics is an essential component of a childhood education. The rate of crime, dishonesty, corruption, and social breakdown around the globe can be attributed to poor and anemic exposure of our children to ethical education. Do not negotiate on the important moral ethical questions. History is series of moral decisions, made or not made. We do nothing in society to identify and reward ethical talent. We are generally governed by "C" grade average students. Magnet schools are developed for math and science. The first citywide magnet school for ethical leadership was developed in San Diego.

More focus on ethics should permeate the educational system and the foundation should begin in the home. You should not cover leadership in your teaching before covering ethics. In the 1960s, there was great self-esteem but no ethics. Avoid logical imbalances in reading. Teach kids not to tolerate "double-speak". Expressions that obscure the real meaning of an idea, such as the "Peacekeeper Nuclear Missile" and "collateral damage" (human victims) should be understood and discounted for what they really are.

Kholberg of Harvard University suggest that children go through certain stages in their understanding of morality and moral reasoning. From his studies, he concluded that children from various international cultures had a common thread of moral development. The stages of his cognitive development theory are as follows:

- Stage 0 is the pre-moral stage and there's no sense of obligation or morality. Too many children in America grow up and never grow out of this stage.

- Stage 1 is the simple authority orientation stage. This is the obedience and punishment model of morality. Obedience to authority and superior power is the motivating force. This stage should be established as early as possible by parents.

- Stage 2 is called the instrumental relativist. "You scratch my back I'll scratch yours" or "an eye for an eye" and exchange-all reciprocity are examples of this model.

- Stage 3 is the interpersonal concordance stage. In this base the child considers his own feelings and the feelings of others. The intentions become important. Empathy is characteristic of this stage.

- Stage 4 is the law-and-order state. This is rigid with fixed rules and hard to change. There is respect for authority and majority rule and post-conventional moral development. Only 20 percent of the adult population may reach this level in their late '20s.

- Stage 5 is the social contract. This is the contractual legalistic orientation.

- Stage 6 is sacrifice for others. Great leaders like Jesus Christ, Martin Luther King and Mahatma Ghandi are examples.

In the ethical continuum of Kholberg, about 4 percent of adults in life reach stage 6 and four percent of adults live life in stage 0. In the great book, The Prince states that "might makes right" and "the end justifies the means." Political systems generally function in stage 2. There's a conflict between ethical integrity at stage 6 and stage 2 of the system. This is the basis of all great films. A stage 3 example is *A Man of All Season* by Beckett. Stage 4 is law and order and an example is the way parents relate to the children. Stage 5 is the social contract. Heroes who suffer for their people are very unique. This is stage 6.

Honesty/ Humility/ Spirituality

Lack of arrogance and the presence of humility and compassion are important components to any value system. Some of my toughest conversations with Mark occurred on the issue of a value system and ethics. When there was a problem or if there were critical issues to discuss, Mark's mother and I played complementary roles. A combination of the tough love and the gentle love approach provided a balance strategy discussing issues and problems. One of us was invariably tough and sometimes uncompromising, and the other pursued the gentle and somewhat yielding approach.

Teaching Mark the importance of right from wrong goes at the core of the value system we tried to stress. We always tried to lead by example. Children do "as you do" more than "as you say."

The importance of ethics in any value system cannot be over-emphasized. The Wall Street scandals of the 1980s clearly demonstrated that high intelligence and a high level of education are not sufficient to succeed in the highly competitive field of business and finance. A highly ethical value system is equally important. Many smart people land in jail. Around the world, corruption is the crippling albatross around the neck of many of the world's societies. Endemic corruption is a poison that grips many communities of the world. The root cause is due to the minimal or negligible focus on ethics in homes and schools.

We focused, like a laser beam, very early on ethics. Of course, children will push rules and standards of behavior to the edge. While this occurs, we should continue the dialogue that brings out the important issues and current situations related to ethics. With Mark, we played a problem-solving game called scenario decision-making. We would propose various situations or problems and asked Mark to solve them, to provide us with his answer. The problems were designed to test this conceptual thinking ability. For example, we might ask, "What would you do if your friend was found to be using drugs and offered you drugs?"

The answer to this question can be very complicated, especially to questions of turning your friend into the authorities. Invariably, a discussion is provided by this type of question, and through the course of the discussion many salient features of both pro and con arguments will come out. These types of exercises build thinking and communication skills. Some ethical issues have no clear reasons why they are right or wrong decisions. Some require deep thought. But they also may require rapid on-the-fly decision-making. Good judgment in complex situations is a superb quality to have. Good judgment is a clear sign of emerging maturity and mental growth. Good judgment is strengthened by the practice that these case simulations can provide.

All the major religions of the world have value systems. This reality has served a very viable function to societies throughout history. Students should begin early to understand and adhere to their value system throughout life. It is a tool for success with a clear conscience.

Risk-taking and decision-making

Critical Issues List

- *No risk no gain*

- *Calculated risk*

- *Examples of reasonable risk*

The old saying goes, "no risk no gain". There is certainly a germ of truth in this statement. In life, many decisions have to be made and a large proportion of the decisions involved taking some level of risk. With risk comes the possibility of failure. We told Mark that he should risk failure in the decisions that he makes. A little failure here and there is not a bad thing. We had him enter various types of contests including tryouts for the international orchestra, various sports teams, and challenging schools. The lessons learned from taking risk and failing are far more valuable than the temporary setback or bad feelings that they might bring if there is failure.

The preferred type of risk-taking in life is calculated risk. This is a risk that has been thoroughly thought through and even discussed with others to get a variety of opinions. Clearly, this is not a whim or an impulsive decision. After a review where advantages and disadvantages are weighed, the decision is made.

Decisions are not permanently written in concrete either. It is perfectly okay to show flexibility and change. On second thought, a change of mind is perfectly acceptable

Middle School Venue

"I must lose myself in action or I'll wither in despair."

—*Anonymous*

American International School, Middle School

Mark's experience in middle school continued in the international school where his grades continued to demonstrate excellence. Because of the Gulf War, Mark had to leave Saudi Arabia for his safety and attend schools in South Carolina and Oregon for a six-month period. During this time, Mark achieved straight A grades in the two schools which he attended in America. We realized then that his preparation at the international school was very good. Mark learned a lot about school and life in America. Unlike his peers in Riyadh, many of the students were less academically oriented.

Mark returned to Saudi Arabia in spring after the Gulf War to finish the academic year. Mark's seventh grade teachers made the following comments about his performance in school. "Mark is enjoyable to have in class, he is pleasant hard-working, and his motivation and attitude are excellent." His geography teacher said that his study skills were strong and his work was neat and accurate. In the eighth grade Mark continued his excellent work and high-performance. His grades reflected his qualities as a student where he had 4 A's and 3 B's. A teacher commented that his study habits were strong and the creative writing teacher said that he was progressing satisfactorily.

Mark benefited from a school that developed a strategic plan. As a part of this strategic plan, the American International School had a mission statement which stated:

> "As a school committed to excellence, we will educate students to be responsible, productive and ethical citizens with the skills to think creatively, reason critically, communicate effectively and learn continuously; we will accomplish this in an American educational environment characterized by high measurable standards and a clearly defined , integrated curriculum, implemented by a superior staff in partnership with parents."

Parents, teachers and administrators of the school developed this strategic plan. The commitment of parents to making their school high quality is clear from this plan. The school reflected in its quality the genuine partnership between parents and the school staff.

Mark continued to make progress in the eighth grade. He ended the year with four A's and 3 B-pluses. His English teacher commented on his good study habits and his algebra teacher mentioned that his math concepts were strong and he exhibited strong class anticipation. His earth sciences teacher said that he was a conscientious student and his history teacher said that his cooperation was excellent. The band teacher commented that he was making good progress in music.

During this time we knew that Mark may be applying for boarding school, therefore, we stressed to him to have strong grades and to prepare for making the application during the ninth grade year. We stressed to him that very good schools would not accept him if his grades were poor. He continued with good study habits that totaled about two hours per day doing homework. He continued his extracurricular activities of music, Boy Scouts and swimming. With good grades we thought his extracurricular activities would position him well for being accepted to a highly selective boarding school.

The time when students are enrolled in middle schools is when they are experiencing the adolescent years. During these teenage years, there can be many distractions based on peer pressure and other major changes going on in a student's life. Mark was able to keep his focus and perform very well during this critical time.

During Mark's ninth grade year, his English teacher labeled him as a conscientious student where he had an A minus for the year. His geometry teacher called him pleasant and hard-working and he earned an A minus. The physical science teacher said that his science concepts were strong and he cooperated well in groups where he earned a B+. His favorite teacher taught him history and at year's end he earned an A minus. The history teacher stated that he showed strong effort and had excellent self-motivation. Mark earned an A in band and the music teacher said that he was a good band member and commented on the strong efforts in his work.

Doing the middle of the ninth grade year Mark applied to four boarding schools and one college. He was accepted to all by the spring of that year. His graduation was a great celebration as he planned to attend Phillips Academy in Andover, Massachusetts in the fall.

Respect Others in a Multicultural World

"To criticize another race or other natural creation is to criticize God who made them."

"There's a nobler ambition than standing up high. It's stooping low to lift another up."

—Anonymous

Critical Issues List

- *Strength through diversity*

- *Tolerance of others*

- *Travel to learn about other cultures*

Relations with others

Mark's heritage is African-Asian-American. America represents the world, and the history of all Americans is very important in understanding the forces that shape the richly colored stain-glass mosaic that is America. America is an idea. The idea, in essence, is " strength through diversity." Native-Americans, African-Americans, European-Americans, Hispanic-Americans, Arab-Americans and Asian-Americans have come to America from all regions of the globe to join one family. Referring to hyphenated Americans does not implicitly divide us, nor does it diminish the reality that we are all Americans. As we reach the beginning of a new millennium, America is unified and, indeed, our diversity symbolizes the planet earth in microcosm.

We are all living in a world with people. The chemistry of our interaction with others determines the quality of our journey during life on planet earth. Our instincts and momentum are toward survival and self-preservation. In a direct way, our feelings of others are limited and are of no apparent relevance. As we mature, we gradually begin to think about others and to consider the importance of their needs.

Key to our relations with others is empathy and it is an expression of this maturity. A mature consciousness of our relations with others elevates us to a higher plane and paves the way through the jungle of life. Empathy and respect should be the pillars of our interactions with others.

Earl E. Guile Sr., Mark's paternal grandfather, said, "If you do not have something good to say about someone, do not say anything." He lived by this precept and he successfully passed it down to his children. It was very simple but effective. It symbolized his view of the way to relate to others.

Each person you encounter has to be judged on his own merits. The stereotypical labeling of entire groups of people should be avoided at all costs. The power of the smile should be harnessed to our advantage. When smiling, our internal systems function better and we cast the ray of warmth to those around us. These are the skills that we need to optimize our relations to the rest of the world.

Mark encountered bias during his formative years. We used the experience to express the idea that in order to overcome racism, you must prepare yourself double or triple the level of the next guy. When someone comes to evaluate you, they should have no doubt that you are the best qualified for the position. During the years when he was in the Boy Scouts, Mark struggled to reach the level of Eagle. He reached the last level before Eagle called Life Scout. Just before the summer that he was leaving for boarding school, he received a letter from the scoutmaster saying that he would not be promoted. He did not give a reason. Mark had completed all the requirements to reach Eagle. A pattern of behaviors led us to believe that this was bias in action. I stressed to Mark that he could not let the feelings of one person defeat him and that he should not show bitterness or hate to the person involved. I encouraged him to continue to pursue his goal of Eagle and we enrolled him in another troop. After transferring his work to the new troop, he met with unbiased leaders and eventually was promoted to Eagle. Mark had overcome an external obstacle in life: racism. He was very happy to reach his goal and learned the valuable lesson that one should persevere in the face of any obstacle in life.

The global village

Historically, culture, geographic barriers, suspicions, and poor communications have separated clans, tribes, nations and ethnic groups. In the late 20th century, as we bridge the millennium, many of the barriers are breaking down. The modern telecommunication revolution is making the world a smaller place. As people who looked different from one another are put together in one place, they have no choice but to interact. Slowly, suspicions are falling and communication is on the upswing. At the end of the cold war, there has been a upsurge in nationalism and ethnic rivalry around the world. Bosnia, Rwanda, India, and Northern Ireland, to name a few, have flared up. The significant countervailing trend is inter-ethnic communication and interaction taking place among young people in the schools of America and across the major cities of Europe. Immigration and trans-national migration have been at the core of this trend. This trend is destined to prevail and the truly educated members of a world society of today and the future will have tolerance and understanding of other people who may not look like them.

Learning from others/ Travel experiences

Extensive travel was one of the unique opportunities that we as a family had living in the Middle East. As an American family living there, we were able to travel back to the United States once a year during summer vacation. This travel afforded us the opportunity to stop in many other countries. We traveled on a round-the-world ticket via our U.S. residence in Portland, Oregon. As long as the travel was in one direction, according to the rules, you could stop in as many cities as possible in an around-the-world itinerary. We therefore visited over 30 countries on four continents.

We view travel for the children as an educational experience. It was just as important as the classroom experience and a child could learn much more in a shorter period of time. I realized it from the beginning that this was a unique opportunity for education. From the time our children were in the first grade, I requested that vacation journals be kept. On all of our trips, at the end of the day, we set aside time for journal writing. We still have many of these journals today and they are hilarious, yet informative, to read. Mark complained at the time but later he viewed that request to write a journal as a very good one.

One of the most important things Mark learned from traveling was the concept of cultural diversity. He learned that there were many different types of people in the world who have their own way of life and way of doing things. He saw this world firsthand when we visited the people on their home turf. There, he saw with his own eyes what life was like—he did not need a textbook to explain things, he could see what was happening directly. I believe that Mark has grown up with the gift for understanding things that are different from himself and for being able to adapt to new circumstances quickly.

Our typical routine when traveling to a new place was as follows: first, we would try to establish a general orientation to the city. After trial and error, we found that the best way to do this was to take a city tour. Through this, we got an expert commentary on the important sites. We also gained a knowledge of the history as it pertains to the city, and we could stake out interesting places to come back later on our own. The children loved that and they would listen intently to the stories and explanations of the tour guide.

For economic reasons, we generally chose 2-and 3-star hotels in most places. Although they got upset, on some occasions, when the hotel was poor, the children accepted the economic style we had to live with. We thought this was also a good lesson for them. Life is not a luxury on all occasions while people around live in poverty. Low-cost but clean hotels brought a sense of reality to our excursions to exotic places.

We relied heavily on guidebooks to show us the major sites in the cities that we visited. Once we established the places we wanted to go from the orientation we would then go back, either walking or by taxi and spend a greater time to understand and appreciate the places we saw. Our children loved that because they could ask questions and wander around, and they could really study the things they saw. It became natural for them to see many cities and experience many new settings. It takes a lot to "wow" them, even to this day. Mark was so used to so many interesting and different things growing up that now he can manage change and new circumstances with ease. We tended to walk a lot in the cities we visited. On many occasions we walked all day. We were all terribly exhausted at night and slept very well, even though in a strange room.

The favorite sites we enjoyed were museums and art galleries. In museums you could behold the best and the most important objects of any society. The descriptions of many items gave subtle insights into the history and the lifestyle of the people. This was a very valuable lesson for Mark, and today after having walked through hundreds of museums, he has a view of the world with a special perspective. We took our time to walk from exhibit to exhibit. We read the inscriptions, and we tried to see as many parts of the museum as possible. In some museums, like The Louvre, in France, it took several days to cover the whole place. Waiting in line to go inside was a problem, sometimes the admission ticket costs were high but it was all worth it, in the context of the educational experience. The costs and efforts were mere tuition for this great education.

There was tremendous bonding between parents and children during these trips. Our travels generally lasted about two months which meant there was enormous quality time spent with the children. During this time we had numerous conversations and discussions about a wide range of topics. After meeting local people in the places we visited we talked to our children about the standard of living and way of life of these people. We discussed that it was important to respect people from all socioeconomic levels and educational backgrounds and never to feel more important than someone else. We took this opportunity to establish a stronger bond between parents and children. Many times we experienced joy, wonder, and amazement. Sometimes these travels led to hardships and inconvenience, but we shared them together.

Our trip to India was a particularly compelling trip because of the great poverty the children there endured. What was very gripping about India was not just poverty, but the extent of it and its intensity. While we were in New Delhi, we traveled by taxi to different parts of the city. As we were heading toward the Red Fort we stopped at a light. Several children, apparently sent by their parents to the streets, came to the window to beg. Because these children were approximately the same age as Mark, he was greatly affected by what he saw. He handed money out of the window to the children. Later, when I asked him about it, I mentioned that he was fortunate to grow up without the need to go out and beg. Mark quietly thought about this point. He did not want to discuss the poverty he saw because he did not want to acknowledge its existence. Later, as he grew older, he actually discussed this incident in some of the essays he wrote in school. When reading those essays, I could then grasp the significance of our trip to India during that summer. What he learned from this experience went even deeper into his thoughts and concerns.

The experience in India and also many other experiences like that in other places were, in my opinion, a very good strategy with the family. Although we made financial sacrifices to travel, it was clearly very important to see the world and see the effect this, great university of learning-through-travel, would have on the children and us.

On several occasions, we traveled by train around Europe with a Euro-rail pass. These trips were particularly fascinating. We set off together in the compartments of European trains and watched the scenery of the continent go by the window. When we reached a town we wanted to visit, we would stop in the railway station and find a place to sit and relax. Sometimes we would find a small cafe across the street. The family would sit with the luggage, while I ventured around in the streets near the railway station to find a hotel. The reason for looking near the station was to provide a convenient way back to board the train for our next destination. The hotels would have a modest price and we would then go, by way of a short walk, to claim a room when I came back. After we freshen up and change, we would then strike out around town to discover the secrets therein. If there was a beach nearby, we would walk to the ocean and observe the scenic beauty of the seashore. Mark's mother would take the opportunity to go shopping when we passed the district of the main stores. This process slowly unveiled a new place to our hearts and our minds. Mark and his brother loved the adventure and they greatly benefited from this sponta-neous type of discovery. This was truly an education that was hard to beat. It's hard to judge the impact of these experiences on a child but I truly believe that the speed and quickness of their adaptability that they have now are the results of these experiences.

On some occasions we traveled on boats. We took a boat, for example, between Stockholm and Helsinki on an overnight trip. Mark became a friend of a young Finnish boy and spent time playing computer games in the arcade on the ship. They wandered all over the ship together over several hours and rapidly became good friends. When we arrived in Turku, Finland, we continued to ride with the boy and his father by train to a city called Tampere, where they showed us interesting sites before they left for the suburbs to return home. This was typical of the kind of travel experience that Mark had, and I believe this helped him learn to make friends quickly in new settings, particularly in a new school.

Journal keeping was a requirement during vacations. The time set aside for writing was after dinner, before bedtime. Although Mark didn't write everyday, he managed to discuss many significant experiences from his perspectives of the time. The journals helped improved his writing and expand his capability to express himself.

This is a travel essay that Mark wrote for one of his school reports.

"Midnight Express" by Taxi

"During the 1992 spring break, I and my family traveled to Greece and Turkey. In Greece we sailed to the island of Rhodes and we had no problems on this particular trip. However, in Turkey, we had a slight problem with returning to Istanbul from the southwest coast.

On April 6th, my family and I were in a town called Pamukkale in southern Turkey. This area is known for its geological wonder with calcium hot springs. It was near the end of the school break and we were trying to get a bus back to Istanbul. All the buses were fully booked with passengers traveling back from the Eid holidays, and we had no idea how to get back to the capital. My father asked around town for possible solutions, two hours later he came up with only one choice. That choice was to take a taxi back through central Turkey to Istanbul, which is approximately eight hundred kilometers away. We left Pamukkale by taxi in the late afternoon. The taxi was a 1980 Renault 12 station wagon that looked like it had been through a lot of "wear and tear." After riding for fifty kilometers, we had the good luck of having a flat tire. It took the taxi driver twenty-five minutes to change the flat tire to the spare which looked worse than the flat tire. An hour and a half later, we passed through a small village and stopped to repair the damaged tire. I noticed that the inner tube of the damaged tire had several patches on it already from previous flats. When the mechanic found the first big puncture in the inner tube, he patched it up. When he tested for other leaks, three more were discovered. The taxi driver gave up on that tube and got another one that had been previously used by someone else. An hour later, we were back on the road to Istanbul. The landscape consisted of trees and hilly patches of barren land. When night fell, the driver started to drive erratically. His unusual and dangerous philosophy was to drive over the median line and shift right when there was oncoming traffic. Between seven and twelve at night, the driver began to get fatigued and my father had to entertain him to keep him awake. They talked about cowboys, Indians, and John Wayne. The driver showed his talent by whistling old western cowboy tunes. Two hours passed and the taxi driver began to talk about the history of Turkey. Around twelve midnight, we pulled over to a rest area for the driver to rest and I climbed in the back of the car on top of the luggage and went to sleep. Two hours later, I was awaken and I crawled back to my seat. We then started again for Istanbul. Around three in the morning, I drifted to sleep again and didn't wake up until 6:30 am. By then, we were in the outskirts of Istanbul. When we arrived at our hotel it was 7:30 am.

This was one taxi ride that I will always remember. The taxi driver probably would not forget it too because of the $250 fare we had to pay him. The total amount of time for our voyage in the cramped taxi was fifteen hours."

Prepare for Change and Eliminate Procrastination/ Developing Activity Lists and Scheduling

"Success means lots of discipline. When Rome stopped disciplining, she started dying. The same holds for 18 other civilizations. If we don't cultivate discipline from within, it will be forced on us from outside. If you have but one gift to leave your children, let it be self-discipline. Without it, they won't be able to handle success, even if it's forced on them."

"Keep a sharp eye on that devil, procrastination, waiting for his chance to lure you to your easy chair, to gossip, to dawdling, and the TV-which is mostly the literature of the illiterate- the amusement of non-thinkers."

"Short as life is, we make it shorter by wasting time."

—Anonymous

Critical Issues List

- *Change means opportunity*

- *The future is not what it use to be*

- *Learn good consistent work habits*

In many project activities children have a tendency to drop out of the activity before momentum is established to acquire a new habit. There are things a parent can do to prevent this problem. Great positive habits, if they are worthwhile, should ideally be established and enjoyed by the child. One technique is to let your child try out various things before making a firm commitment. This can be done by making arrangements with instructors, who are coordinators of the program, to allow your child to go for one week to see how he likes it. One week is not enough time to develop a habit but it certainly can let your child experience whether he would or would not enjoy the activity. You can then avoid making a financial commitment for an instrument or for some equipment that may be required for this activity.

When the child begins an activity, you should look for minor signs of progress. When these are found, give praise lavishly. Don't expect quick progress and expert levels early. Some activities take a lot of skill and to reach that skill level requires a lot of time. The activities should always be looked upon as fun. Don't impose your desire to be in a particular activity on your child. Also don't impose your standards and ideas of perfection on your child. If the child wants to quit, sit down and have a discussion about the whole idea. You must encourage him to continue with the activity for awhile to see if this perception may change. Avoid judgmental statements about your child's desires. Respect the child's view and develop a method for discussing his frustrations. If the child continues to insist on quitting, have him present this plan to the teacher or coach. Your child may even change his mind at this point after being persuaded by the coach. But if he doesn't, he should defend his position successfully. At least, he will learn a lesson from this experience. Coercion should be avoided because this method can backfire and create anger and resentment in the child. Also, parents should not live vicariously through their children.

Dealing with homework

Critical Issues List

- *Establish a good environment*
- *Set definite time for homework*
- *Provide guidance*

The best plan with homework is to establish a good environment for it to be done. The environment and location are important for successfully establishing the work ethic to complete homework. Find a quiet place and close off the rest of house, if it's possible. A peaceful, calm environment is necessary. Also, of course, the rest of the family should not disturb the child while he is working on homework.

There should be a definite time for homework. Preferably, this should be the same time everyday. There should be a gradual increase in this time as a child gets older, to allow him to complete all of the assignments in the allotted time. Give a minimum amount of time to work. If he finishes before this minimum time, he should be encouraged to read other books until the time is up. If it takes too long to finish, set up deadlines and have him try to finish before a pre-established time. This challenge is, to the child, a game. Always praise the child for any work he does. This should be done on a daily basis. Children love praise and are highly motivated by it.

A parent should not do the homework. The child will develop discipline and self-satisfaction when he does it himself. Parents should merely provide guidance for the child. The help should focus on explaining fundamental principles and methods, like a teacher, but not doing problems or writing reports.

Research indicates that homework given to children before middle school does not enhance achievement. Over 100 studies suggest that the effect of homework on elementary educational achievement is trivial. It was found further that homework, especially large quantities, was positively associated with a poor attitude toward school. Good homework at this stage was found to be short and easy to complete quickly. By middle school though students were found to get great benefits from homework. This was usually linked to the homework being focused, creative, and imaginative. The child generally has more stamina at this time and is old enough to see the possible application of the new knowledge.

Prepare for change in the 21st century

Find out what you need to know and relentlessly pursue it, then use it. What distinguishes successful people from those who are not is that successful people find the pertinent knowledge and relentlessly use it. The quantity of knowledge is doubling every five years, therefore it is impossible to keep up and know everything.

The best time to search for knowledge and to apply it is now. Profound change is the constant in our lives. Furthermore, change is accelerating. The Chinese character for change has a double meaning—danger and opportunity. Change can be very dangerous if we're not prepared for it, but it represents a unique and powerful opportunity for those who have the insights and eye sights to spot the opportunity.

Organize your workspace

Critical Issues List

- *Establish a student office*
- *Plan your work on a daily basis*

- *Avoid time destroyers*

- *Break larger tasks down to smaller tasks*

Organizing your work areas and getting the critical resources can help prepare you for success. Working smart is far more important than working hard. Organize the resources that are needed to accomplish your school work. The following are central components of a student office.

1.   Desk with adequate lighting in a quiet area

2.   File cabinet

3.   Pencil and paper

4.   Bound notebooks for each class

5.   Computer with a CD-ROM and Internet access

6.   Dictionary and other reference books

7.   Planning book and calendar

Plan the work on a daily basis. Record all homework assignments in a dated planner. This should be a constant reference for you to determine what and when your assignments have to be prepared; also you can plan your study time for upcoming exams if you take the time to record accurate information.

Establish a daily planning list. List all of your important classes and make a note of what you need to do before class to prepare for it. In this way you can avoid being called on and not being prepared. Prioritize your list. Take any spare moments and head to the library for further preparation.

When you have work to do, don't be tempted to waste your time because others have time to waste. Be strict with yourself, and plan later your time for relaxing and goofing off. That's important too. It, however, must be short and sweet, and at a time after your study commitments. The friends will begin to respect you for your business-like approach to school and work. They certainly can increase your viable friendships, but mainly on your time and terms.

Establish friendships with those who are inclined to have the same work ethic and seriousness about study that you have. This does not suggest that you exclude others for friendships. Find classmates who are interested in forming a study group for a particular subject. As a team, you can set aside time before exams with a chalk board and systematically go over problems and concepts together. This measure is powerful and takes on its energy of its own. Reports indicate that students are more efficient in the use of time by this team approach and everyone benefits. If you organize this group, it can provide viable leadership experience. Coordinating and compromising over differences of opinion and organizing the logistics are important skills to learn.

Take a large task and break it down to smaller tasks. This is a piece-meal solution for any job. If you need to finish a meal, you do that by taking one bite at a time. If you have ever to reach the top of the stairs, you generally take one step at a time. This very simple idea can be applied to daily tasks, and we can subsequently reduce the proverbial mountains to plains. A long-term paper should be divided into specific workable components. Work alone in sections and build transitions to pull the individual components together. It's almost magical how large projects can be tamed by this psychological trick of piece-meal work strategy.

Start now, don't wait until the last minute. Pick up tools and go to work now. Gather things needed for a project in one place. Then take those items, one by one, and put them to work. If they are references for your manuscript take notes from them, in preparation for putting these ideas in your manuscript. For a set of math problems calculate on a scrap paper and begin to solve the problems, one by one, until you're finished. Don't waste time, go directly to the task and do it. As the Nike ads say, "Just do it."

Let's review the definition of procrastination.

pro.cras.ti.nate vb -nat.ed ; -nat.ing [L procrastinatus, pp. of procras-tinare, fr. pro-forward + crastinus of tomorrow, fr. cras tomorrow] vt (1588): to put off intentionally and habitually ∼ vi: to put off intention-ally the doing of something that should be done syn see delay—

Establishing a schedule

Critical Issues List

- *Take inventory of your present work habits by keeping a diary of what you do from hour to hour in the course of the day*

- *Establish planning and scheduling as a regular part of your work routine*

- *Set aside the total hours on a daily basis for study in your schedule*

- *Find a special place for your routine study with a comfortable light and pleasant environment*

- *Go over your lecture notes on a daily basis/ Copy notes over to a notepad*

- *Plan regular rest breaks during study*

Perhaps the most difficult aspect of study is developing the habit of sit-ting for an expanded period of time and accomplishing a task. Through the ages, all manners of ideas have been applied to this simple problem. Crucial to the success of a student is the establishment of a regular habit of sitting in a place and carrying out the task of study. Many children study when they feel inspired or when the work is due at the last minute. This haphazard approach has a major disadvantage because no clear patterns of behavior are established. It was our view as parents that we had to help establish these patterns of behavior in our children. Scheduling is a very important approach to organizing time and becoming more productive.

Much of the research indicates that by aged 15, habits are fairly well established regarding how a student studies. If those habits are poor, they will surely make it difficult for that student to manage rigorous academic workloads. Many students who go to college find that they have to scramble to organize themselves because the workload demands disciplined study, a skill they do not have.

The planning of your time is a critical habit that must be formed. We stressed to Mark the necessity of scheduling his daily activities. The habits that we instilled in him at a young age continue to the present. In modern life there are many things competing for our time. There is, of course, television, socializing, sports, and generally having a good time. The demands of the academic responsibilities should be paramount in the mind of the student. This is priority number one. The other demands on our time are very important for the well-balance individual and for general growth and development, but they should always be understood as second priority.

Parents should follow their instincts when advising their children on the use of time. Shift the decision-making within a general framework to the student. It's very important for a student to make his own decisions about the scheduling of his time. Schedules and demands should not be forced without discussion and debate. Ideally, courses of action should be mutually agreed upon and the student should develop the specifics. This strategy ensures that he would adhere to the decision and follow through more readily. In the regular working world, one is required to be at the job from 9 to 5. There are requirements for specific work to be done, and the employee must follow a schedule that is established by someone else. The difference between the employee and the student is that the student must establish a schedule himself. If the schedule is not established, much time is wasted with indecision and lack of motivation. A schedule establishes a pattern and it becomes the norm. If students know that they must work between such and such hours doing math, they will follow this objective. With Mark, we tried a standard schedule in his early educational years, and he built on this concept through ninth grade. By that time, it became a habit for him to sit down at a regular scheduled time to do his academic work. On some occasions, he would have a sports activity scheduled. The most important thing we observed was the establishment of a habit pattern which became the norm.

There are many distractions that children have to deal with as they are growing up. In some environments, a child is engaged in leisure activities for much of the time outside of school. The peer pressure to play and not spend time studying is very strong. There is also a problem with television. The enormous number of hours that a student spends watching TV can be crippling to the academic performance. It is therefore very important that TV watching, computer games, excess of leisure, and other distractions be managed successfully.

During holidays we were flexible in the scheduling. However, we took advantage of this time to see an activity schedule in operation during a full day. For balance, the leisure time was scheduled and we added some academic work to keep the momentum of scholarship flowing. This also permitted the exploring of new subjects of study, such as astronomy, geography and art. Some schedules filled out expanded holiday periods. In the beginning Mark did not enjoy the schedules but he later developed the skill to write them up himself. He was able to accomplish certain milestones during the time allocated in his schedule.

Before establishing an activity schedule, it is important to take inventory of how time is utilized at the present. The students should keep a diary of what they do in the course of a typical day. All of the activities should be analyzed to determine how efficient the use of time is made. An important goal is to establish a viable, workable schedule. We did this very early when Mark was quite young in elementary school and found that there was considerable wasting of time. We developed a more productive schedule, which had a balance toward a variety of activities and was not rigid and inflexible.

There are questions that should be asked when looking at how your time is used. The most important questions are, "Are you spending enough time studying? Is there enough time on task? Is time being wasted on something which results in no productivity? Is there a balance between leisure and work activities? Can the time, as presently utilized, be used more efficiently?" Schedule planning should be done on a weekly basis. Flexibility and the ability to change the schedule are very important. However, the establishment of the ideal schedule is key. A routine of scheduling is the precursor for establishing even longer-range goals and plans.

How much study does the average student need? This question is highly linked to the year of studies and the rigor of the school where the student is studying. At a very young age, such as six or seven, a parent should start with a modest amount of studying time for the child (1/2 hour to one hour). As the child gets older, the time should gradually be increased to help the child adapt to work and concentration. This is very important; over time, the habit of steady study becomes well established for the child. We commonly set for Mark a certain amount of time after school for study. We found that we would generally organize work to be accomplished during this time. When he could not finish we merely expanded the time so that he could. The important process underway was developing the discipline of sitting at a desk for an extended time in order to accomplish a given task. When he was tired of sitting and concentrating, we were very flexible about taking breaks. Typically, he would leave his study even if he was not finished and go to swim practice. This was a sports-and-exercise break that energized him and transported him to an entirely different activity. After swim practice, he would finish any homework that was remaining. As the workload grew over the years, we gradually set different hours for him to study. By the time he reached the upper grades, where large amounts of homework were required, he was conditioned and adapted to sitting at the desk and accomplishing his tasks successfully. We meticulously avoided letting him stay up late to study. We felt sleep was very important in order to be prepared and alert the next day in classes. Therefore, we established early bed times which gradually also changed as he grew older.

Most research indicates that energy levels decline late in the day and in the evening. We would, for example, concentrate on having them finish this main intellectual work in the afternoon after school, before the activities began. Most curves of efficiency indicate that work is more efficient in early morning hours. We stressed early morning hours for accomplishing intellectual tasks when there was no school. The afternoons could then be devoted to sports and play.

Taking rest periods were very important. Even short breaks, 5 or 10 minutes, were considered viable because the stop re-energized and helped him be fresh for continued concentration. Sometimes just getting up, stretching, and taking a walk through the house or digging up a snack in the refrigerator were excellent things to do during brief rest periods.

Scheduling

A typical schedule of activities Mark formulated during parts of vacation periods (7th grade).

(This was a framework for activities and not a strict unbending agenda)

1. Breakfast 8 a.m. to 8:30 a.m.

2. Reading on the couch 8:30 a.m. to 9:00 a.m.

3. Math on the computer 9 a.m. to 9:30 a.m.

4. SAT studying 9:30 a.m. to 9:45 a.m.

5. Read CD-ROM 9:45 a.m. to 10 a.m.

6. Watch laserdisc 10 a.m. to 10:30 a.m.

7. Read on couch 10:30 a.m. to 11:00 a.m.

8. Break for eating lunch 11:00 to 1:00 pm.

9. SAT studying 1:00 p.m. to 1:15 p.m.

10. Read a book of my choice 1:15 p.m. to 2:00 p.m.

11. Typing 2:00 to 2:30 p.m.

12. Various 2:30 to 3:00 p.m.

13. Done 3:00 p.m.

An annotated schedule Mark designed (circa 7th grade).

1. Breakfast I first getup wash-up, brush my teeth, go downstairs to eat whenever I want.

2. I'd choose a book: one I like or an assigned book and read for half-hour.

3. Turn on a computer and do a section on math.

4. Take the SAT book and read the sections today for 15 minutes.

5. Look up subjects on the CD-ROM. For example encyclopedia and I read it.

6. Watch laserdisc programs on the computer and do a 100 word essay.

7. I rest, eat, play around and read

8. Same as item before

9. Getting a book of my choice and reading for 45 minutes on the couch or the bed

10. Do a typing lesson today using master type and typing tutor

11. Various project

12. Done, stop, play, TV

High School Venue

"Our greatest need is to teach people how to think—not what, but HOW."

—*Edison*

Phillips Academy, Andover, MA

When Mark reached the end of the ninth grade there was no more high school available in Saudi Arabia. Out of necessity we had to send him back to North America for his studies. We considered sending him to public high school. We also explored sending him to a high school of science and technology. Most of these schools had residency requirements that made it difficult to qualify to attend. He eventually applied and was accepted to the Science Academy of Austin, Texas. After further investigation he decided to apply to what many call the best high schools in America, the northeastern preparatory schools.

His previous attendance to the Phillips Exeter Academy summer school made him familiar with the system and quality of these schools. He applied to Choate Rosemary Hall, Hotchkiss, Phillips Academy, and to Phillips Exeter. His academic credentials were good and he presented with excellent extracurricular experience in swimming, music, and the Boy Scouts. These applications were in many ways like college applications and these particular schools were highly selective in choosing their students for matriculation. Mark was successful in gaining admission in all of the northeastern schools he applied to as well as the Science Academy of

Austin. He also applied to Morehouse College in Atlanta, Georgia, because they had a special early admission program. He fortunately, had taken the SAT exam with a respectable score and this qualified him for admission to college from the ninth grade. With all these choices on the table, making a final decision was difficult and soul searching. It was tempting to forego high school and begin immediately with college education, but after careful thought Mark decided not to follow this course because it might be premature. Instead, he decided to accept a position at Phillips Academy, in Andover, Massachusetts. The screening process of getting in at Andover was very difficult. They accepted only 20 percent of the applicants who applied from all over the world.

This decision led him to attend what many consider one of the top high schools in America. It was founded in 1778 and is the oldest private high school in the country. The motto of the school in Latin "non sibi," means "not for self". The school also has a constitution, which states that it will prepare "youth from every quarter." The school states:

"The school's constitution, written in 1778, states that Andover 'shall be ever equally open to youth of requisite qualification from every quarter.' With this principle in mind the basic requirement for admission to Andover today continues to be evidence of sound character and strong academic achievement. The school is especially interested in candidates who demonstrate independence, maturity and concern for others, in addition to high performance in particular studies or activities. Valuing diversity in its student body, the school seeks to bring together a community from all parts of the country and from many nations."

The statement of purpose…

"…The academy's scholastic program is designed to foster excellence in all disciplines associated with the liberal arts tradition. Faculty members guide students to master skills, to acquire knowledge, and to think critically, creatively and independently. The school strives to help young people achieve their potential not only in intellectual understanding, but also in aesthetic sensitivity, physical well-being, athletic prowess and moral decisiveness so that they may lead productive, responsible lives. Committed to discovering authentic sources of community the academy strives to understand and respect the difference that arise in a multicultural setting."

Mark began his career at Andover in his tenth grade year. His overall experience at Andover can be summarized in one sentence—-it was hard work and tremendous growth. During this three-year period Mark had to endure and adjust to a quantum leap in academic intensity. At first, he suffered a serious drop in his grades. This gave rise to some concern, but slowly he made the necessary adjustment and began to show improvement in his grades. His homework time expanded from 2 hours per school day to over 5 hours per day. This intensity of Andover was something that caught Mark and us by surprise. The brilliant students around also humbled him. In the past he had been near the top of his class and in Andover he was in the middle of the pack. Fortunately, Mark had a nurturing elementary and middle school experience. The balance was just about right to avoid burnout and to avoid being under challenged. There was a joy of learning, nurturing, and foremost fun in this early phase that built the foundation. From this foundation Mark was prepared to make the adjustment to the increased intensity after the drop in his grades and showed steady improvement after the first year. His persistence and his attitude of success carried him through.

In extracurricular activities, Mark continued to thrive in swimming and music by making the varsity swim team and joining the school band to play the baritone. In swimming, Mark achieved high self-esteem at a time when it was virtually destroyed by the difficulty of the academic program. In spite of this, Mark pursued an advanced mathematics track which put him a year ahead of most of his peers. He achieved this foundation earlier with extra math studies during his middle school years.

By the second year, Mark's grades improved dramatically as he adapted to the new system and began to enjoy his highly trained teachers. His pre-calculus teacher, for example, had finished his Ph.D. at MIT. Mark performed well in science and math. He achieved his highest grades at Andover in those subjects. It was during these three years when Mark came in contact with many superb students who had ambition to go to highly selective colleges that his goal in that direction crystallized. It was during these years that he made initial contact with the college counseling office at Andover.

We found, as parents, that this office which advises students on matters concerning college admissions is one of the most important and most effective offices in the school. The counselors provided complete and highly professional advice on preparing for college admission. This was critically important for Mark's success with his college applications. They provided expert advice on all the elements of college admissions. They also provided step-by-step monitoring of all phases of what they call the college admission season, between the junior and the senior year. The colleges appreciate the work of the college counselors office because they know that an application coming from Andover will be complete and a joy to read. The work of this office alone is justification enough for a family to consider sending a child to boarding school.

Although boarding school is not for every student, it offers a unique college level of education and academic responsibility at a younger age. The transition to college is much smoother for students who experience boarding school. If a family and student feel that they would benefit from this early maturing experience away from home, they should investigate boarding school. The highly regarded *Peterson's Guide to Private Secondary Schools in the USA and Abroad* provides complete information on numerous private schools all around the country.

The classic questions that a family asks about an academically rigorous boarding school are, " Should my child go to Hometown High and possibly be valedictorian or should he go to Phillips Academy and end up in the middle of the pack? Which strategy will get him accepted to the most selective colleges?" There is no correct answer to these questions but we found that the quality of the education was more important than the rank in the class. We also felt that selective colleges recognize the quality of the education at Andover and admits their graduates at a greater rate than they do for Hometown High graduates.

Financially, private schools are a burden to the average family. Many of these private high schools, including Andover, have over 75% of their students benefiting from financial aid. Many of the schools stressed that finances should not be a barrier to applying for private school. It would be a good exercise for a student to go through the application process and gain experience that prepares him for the college application process a few years later.

The proof of Mark's success at Andover was his success in gaining admission to 13 highly selective colleges. Mark had a long-standing interest in attending MIT and therefore elected to matriculate there for the fall of 1996.

Plan Your Education Future

"If you have a dream, you have everything that matters. If you have no dream, it's later than you think. Better get one."

—Anonymous

Critical Issues List

- *Think ahead about college*

- *Find out what the college expects of you*

- *Plan your educational future*

Think ahead about college

Family talk should begin as early as elementary school about future colleges. High ideals and the very best of education should be the targets your children aim for. Social economic status is no barrier to higher education in selective colleges. Even the poorest members of society can earn full scholarships to the most selective colleges because of the policy of needs blind admission. This means that applicants are evaluated for their academic and special talents, irrespective of their capacity to pay college costs. Once they are accepted, the financial aid office begins awarding financial aid according to need. The critical hurdle is to get accepted by the admissions committee.

In order to prepare for this hurdle, it is essential to think way ahead. If an elementary student begins to dream about the universities they want to attend, a great effort and labor over many years may just be possible. The vision has to be there. Parents are important in instilling the motivation and desire.

We talked about college very early. We stressed the importance of education to help one achieve success in life. We visited college campuses when we got the chance. During those visits, we talked about the great difficulty in getting accepted to those colleges. The seeds were planted.

I encouraged Mark to look at college view books and catalogs. It might seem unusual, but if approached the right way, young children can take an interest in these matters. By just having these books around, they are bound to have influence on the thinking of the student.

Researching the reasons for success, a large study looked at the common factors among extraordinarily successful people from various cultural backgrounds. The most important common thread was the presence of a large quantity of books around the house. Subscribing to this theory, getting the books about selective colleges may be critically helpful in stimulating the student to work and prepare for the great challenge ahead of matriculating at selective schools.

Looking at the materials for the colleges gives a student chance to find out what the colleges expect from him. If the student finds out that special skills and knowledge in at least one area is required, he can begin very early in acquiring those skills. Music practice, an early head start in a sport, and special courses in creative writing are the results of pursuing long-term goals.

It should be stressed that activities are not initiated merely to satisfy and impress admissions officers. Activities are pursued because the student is genuinely interested in them. This genuine interest and dedication over several years are what truly benefit the growth and development of the child. The viable byproduct is the attention it gets to the college of your choice.

Henry Rosovsky the former Dean of Students at Harvard described the admission process in selective universities around the world as follows.

"In many parts of the world, the choices could be made by computer; an entrance examination consisting entirely of academic subjects is used to rank applicants and the number for vacancies determines those admitted, the first to the last. The is essentially how it is done by each university in Japan…"

Dr. Rosovsky stated further with regard to the admissions process in American universities the following:

"…Selection procedures in elite American institutions are very different. While objective criteria such as test scores and grades play a major role, they tend to be supplemented by subjective, qualitative, non-quantifiable, and personal components. I would describe the procedures as an exercise in social engineering, involving high school grades, essays, interviews, recommendations from teachers, and above all a general vision concerning the composition of an ideal freshman class. The ideal is most easily defined as an optimum degree of diversity—hence my allusion to Noah's Ark—with a framework of academic excellence, thereby maximizing the opportunity for students to learn from each other. The desired degree and type of diversity will differ from place to place and time to time. I will attempt to describe the most important classes that are considered today in private universities. Most of these will apply without modification to selective independent colleges and some are also considered by public universities."

Part II

Strategies for Excellence

Stress Academic Skills / Challenge Yourself Through Your Courses

"One success formula: Bite off more that you can chew, then chew it. If you have the "can do" it will create the " how to."

—Anonymous

Critical Issues List

- *Take a demanding course-load*

- *Improve your writing skills*

- *Improve your research paper writing skills*

- *Improve your mathematics skills*

- *Learn from Bloom's taxonomy*

Take a demanding course-load

In a recent Newsweek article entitled "The Rat Race Begins At 14," it was pointed out that the pressures are increasing for students to perform at an intense level in high school to gain acceptance in the top colleges. Due to the increasing importance of Advanced Placement exams, SAT tutoring has turned college preparation into a four-year nightmare. Alfie Kohn, the author of the book, *No Contest: The Case Against Competition* says that "school is no longer about learning. It's merely about credentialing." One student countered by suggesting that her parent's investment of $1500 for a SAT tutor and her getting up at 4:00 a.m. for studying extra time helped to get her in Stanford as an early decision student. Julie Schoknecht, a varsity volleyball player, has no regrets about the hard work. She is happy she made the sacrifice to get in her favorite college.

Students like Julie are increasingly pushing themselves in the context of the increasing competition. At New Trier High, in Illinois, students are not satisfied with the 8:10 a.m. to 3:20 a.m. schedule. Many students opt for extra classes in science and music that begin as early as 7:00 a.m. and many of them study well past midnight. Many of the students say they thrive on the competition. This is a new trend in America. In many foreign countries, tutors, extra school, and intense competition are the norms. In a country like India, the prestigious IIT or Indian Institute of Technology, India's MIT, gets 200,000 applications of superbly qualified students for only 2000 places. In Turkey, the national exams require students to attend a cram school after the regular school if there is any hope of attending a Turkish University. In Japan, the notorious university examinations are called "examination hell." Mothers move to distant cities from home to have their sons attend a cram school and prepare for university exams. Some of the mothers even attend the classes with their children. Enormous sums are invested in the preparation of their children. This intensity sometimes takes its toll on some of the kids. They get pushed over the edge by this system. Some of these situations reach unnecessary extremes. Parents have to be cautious and keep a balance.

Some authorities, including college admission people, are worried about the trend. A psychiatrist, Dr. David Fassler says that you do not need a big name college to be a success in life and that many students are devastated when they do not reach their goal. It could be said that preparing for excellence is not inherently a bad thing when a child does not reach his goal. It better prepares him for life. Even if he fails he will be at a high level of achievement and ability and will have momentum for future success. In other words, failure is not necessarily a bad thing. If students do not prepare for the top colleges they are guaranteed not to get in those as well as other less selective schools.

Take the toughest courses offered by your school. In high school students, college admission officers look for evidence of difficult and challenging courses in your program.

Try to take at least one honors course each semester between the ninth and twelfth grade. Honors courses are designated as Advanced Placement (AP) courses or college level courses. The selective college looks to see if a student will seek out a challenge and optimally utilize the resources of a school available to him.

Many students ask, " would a grade of A in a non-honors course be respected more than a grade of B or B- in an honors course? " There is no firm definitive answer to this question, but admission officers lean toward giving more weight to lower grades in the honors course. The most selective colleges look for A's in the honors courses. MIT states, " We encourage you to take the most challenging courses available. Most of our applicants are able to take difficult courses and receive A's."

The quality of high schools vary from town to town and from city to city. If a student comes from a weak high school, high grades on an AP test in a subject area commands respect from a selective college. Regarding the question of whether MIT takes into account that some secondary schools offer more rigorous programs and have tougher grading, it states:

"Yes. We know that there are some schools with very strict grading standards in which few students receive As. We also know that there are some schools that offer little in the way of AP or advanced course preparation. The admissions staff is concerned with the extent to which the student has challenged him- or herself in the context of the high school and if he or she is capable of handling the academic rigors of MIT."

It is possible that grades will suffer in the beginning but experience and exposure will enhance a student's ability to cope with difficult subject matter. The bottom line at a selective college is to choose students who can handle the severe and heavy work load. It's unfair to the student to have his hopes and ambition crushed by a tough curriculum at a selective college. The psychological trauma can be great.

The advantage of taking an AP course also relates to the national standards established. For each subject, national guidelines on course content and the national exams, given after the course, insure standardization. Study aids are numerous and extensive; and there are computer programs to assist the student. Even a weak student can improve dramatically with all the assistance available.

The old adage used to describe the best three factors in real estate value are : "location, location, location." In gaining admission to selective colleges, the three most important criteria are : " transcript, transcript, transcript." The quality of the transcript will make or break most applications. Students have to start early in their academic careers and make their transcripts strong and impressive.

An AP course in calculus is a great way to establish a good mathematical foundation in high school. An AP English course can prepare a student to have more effective writing skills. These skills will help to promote high scores on the SAT exams, thus strengthening the student's profile in several categories.

The grades that are earned in the junior year and the first semester of the senior year carry the greatest weight. The colleges are especially interested in an improving trend in your grade performance.

After AP classes be sure to take the national administered AP test in a given subject. Selective colleges do not require these courses, but a high grade of 4 to 5 is very impressive and boasts the applicant's strength.

If your school is reluctant to allow a student to enroll in an AP course, parents should visit the school and argue the case for their child. Inactive and passive parents can send the wrong message to the school and hinder the child's chances. Students from minority backgrounds have faced this problem for years. They have been discouraged from taking AP courses. Those students who insist become more formidable and competitive when the college admission season arrives.

This is the recommended MIT high school preparation for admission:

One year of high school physics

One year of high school chemistry

One year of high school biology

Math through calculus

A foreign language

Four years of English

Two years of humanities, social sciences

Improve your reading skills

The importance of reading cannot be over-emphasized in the education of a child. Our early strategy was to teach Mark at an early age to read, before he was exposed to formal schooling. This paid off tremendously in his behalf. Once he learned how to read at 3 years of age, he began to explore the wonderful world of books. We made a point to stretch imagination and his thinking by gradually exposing him to more and more complex material. We exposed him to books over his head and beyond his level of comprehension. Through this progressively more complex exposure, Mark's ability to read grew and his desire to explore flourished.

There are many types of reading that one must consider when developing a reading list. Some delegated reading is the search for specific information. Other reading is exploratory and is a survey of knowledge. There is reading to review material that has been covered in the past. And there is reading which is primarily for enjoyment. The last area of reading is the tying together of material into a synthesis from various manuscripts. A capable and strong reader should be skilled in all these types of reading.

A recent study of the National Education Goals Panel that tracked children to see if they were ready to learn found huge learning gaps. Few parents read to their children, and most do not teach them how to read. The percentage of children 3 years or younger who have their parents reading to them is only 45%. Those in the 3-to-5-year groups the percentage is 56%. This is highly related to the educational level of the parents where 73% of college graduates read to their 3-to-5-year-old children daily. This timetable is very important because the period from birth to age three is critical for hard wiring of a verbal learning capability to the brain. If parents do not pass on these critical skills at this early age, they leave their children struggling in elementary school. These scientific studies are important because they tell us what is important to do and the age periods that are critical to provide the proper teaching and learning environment. The mantra should be, "stimulate, stimulate, stimulate for maximum success."

When children learn how to read they go through several distinct phases. The first stage is call reading readiness. This is characterized by an intellectual and physical readiness. The eyesight and hearing must be good. This generally begins at three and reaches the optimum time when the child attends first grade.

In the second stage, the child begins to read very simple materials and learns a stable basic vocabulary of about 100 to 500 words.

During the third stage, the vocabulary of the child builds rapidly. Partly during this time, the child begins to use reading as a practical advantage for learning new things about the world.

The fourth stage demonstrates a refinement of all of the skills learned in the previous three stages. The child begins to read effectively and rapidly. This is the time that parents should really capitalize on this new skill and provide ample reading material for the child to consume. This is a particularly important time to go to a library and establish the habit of using library books and reading to the child on a regular daily basis. It is the job of the standard education system to carry the child through the four stages of reading. Parents can initiate this process, well before formal schooling begins so the child can have a head start.

The reading readiness phase is generally the base for reading, through which all children normally passes. It is very important that parents read to their children daily. Establish the habit so that the child will not let you put him to bed without reading to him first.

We read to Mark nearly every night as he grew up. I read difficult books with more advanced ideas in order to begin stretching his thinking. One book I recall that gave him difficulty was *Zen and the Art of Motorcycle Maintenance*. This book while discussing the journeys of a father with his son by motorcycle around the United States also had a philosophical theme that flowed through the book. Mark enjoyed the adventure and descriptive travel parts of the book but found great difficulty in the beginning with the examination of philosophy. This generated considerable discussion about the book and stimulated interest in topics that were beyond his comprehension at the time. I could tell by the gleam in his eyes that the time we set for reading was very special. It certainly inspired me to continue with this habit after seeing the effects on him.

We also began a habit that I acquired from my mother of reading interesting excerpts from articles that I discovered during the course of the day. I would stop wherever we were and begin reading parts of an article. This habit, while sometime annoying to children, was something they grew use to. Invariably, a discussion would emerge out of a point made, and it would give me a chance to play our scenario game of problem-solving.

While riding in the car we would reverse the role sometimes. As he grew older, I would have Mark read to me. This, as with other requests, was protested in the beginning but later developed into a habit that Mark felt comfortable with. He would read interesting passages to me, and I would take the time to discuss the ideas presented and to pose problems that I asked Mark to solve. I felt that these early experiences of reading and discussing issues vigorously provided the foundation for Mark to develop strong problem-solving skills. This also helped him to develop an intense curiosity about the world and stimulated him to read more.

I could see that Mark was moving through the stages of reading before the elementary level. Although some parents choose to wait for formal schooling to initiate the reading process, we chose to begin early. In anything that we begin early, we always weighed carefully the question of pushing things too fast. In the case of reading, we thought that if he enjoyed the stimulation and the discussion in the process, why not let him continue so that he would indeed be stimulated and happy.

Key to our efforts in teaching him how to read was the use of a phonics approach to the process. We found an excellent phonics book that became invaluable in our teaching game. Once the process began we found Mark rapidly progressing through the third stage characterized by a rapid increase in vocabulary. Mark began to see now how this gain could expand his universe. Everyday the progress encouraged us, as parents, to continue along our chosen pathway. We knew that the efforts we used to stimulate him intellectually were paying off huge dividends in progress, enthusiasm, and wonder.

By the time he blossomed in the Montessori program, we saw him enter the fourth stage of reading. We saw refinement of his skills and the implementation of this new possibility in a wide variety of ways. As we drove along the roads and streets, Mark would read to us the signs that he understood. He was beginning to understand the world around him.

In retrospect, I see this period of him learning to read, prior to any formal schooling, as having been a key foundation that was established. The bricks of that foundation were solid, and they prepared him to build a wonderful house of intellectual achievement in the future.

Improve your writing skills

Critical Issues List

The road toward excellent writing:

- *How often do you have your child write?*

- *What kind of writings do they do?*

- *How much first draft writing do they do?*

- *Let them use log books to track their writing? What kind of responses are they getting and making toward their writings?*

- *What is your child being taught about writing in school?*

In writing across the curriculum, according to Dr. Margaret Healy from the University of California at Berkeley, there is a link between language and learning. We, as parents, must take advantage of this link when promoting learning and language with our children. Language is a medium of learning. Very few parents put special emphasis on language in teaching their children. In a book called *Language and Learning* by James Britain he said, "language is the exposed edge of thought." We can use writing to help our children think and learn. The writer that looks inward is the writer that organizes. I know what I'm thinking about when I see what I have written. Writing is an aid to learning. How does writing help you learn? Writing proves that you have learned something, especially when you have explained it in a clear, simple, and precise way.

Generative writing is a method to teach our children to write. You begin to write and in the course of writing you find out whether you understand something. This writing is tentative, the purpose is discovery and it links new information with old information. Does this snowball of learning get large? No. It stays the same size but it is continuously reorganized. Children must constantly reorganize their understanding. We use language to represent the world. This is our world. We must use language in a productive way.

Many people use the dump truck theory of writing—information is taken from some place and dumped to another. This is different from creative writing where the creative process blossoms. We should not put too much emphasis on neatness when teaching our children to write. We should teach them words and later sentences and still later paragraphs, which ultimately are put together to become compositions.

It is best to begin writing with an idea. Tell your child to start with wanting to say something. Delay emphasis on corrections and perfection. Do not have your child generate words on paper and correct them right away. Let him do what professional writers do and postpone corrections.

One strategy suggested by James Wilder is to read to your children for six months before letting them write. This reading should be replete with a wide variety of materials and writings. Scientific writing, fiction, nonfiction, as well as textbook presentations should be read to the child.

The writing process is composed of pre-writing, drafting, responding, revising, rewriting, editing, reading, evaluation, and publishing. Arthur Applebee suggests that only two stages are involved in the writing process. Those stages are reading and evaluation. There's generally no emphasis on pre-writing or drafting. That is ironic because pre-writing is the most important stage of writing. The items critical to rewriting are discussion of a topic with others, reading about the topic, listening to someone talk about the topic, and brainstorming with yourself or with others on the question. Teach your child how to find something to write about. Show him the power of the draft. A very good exercise is to write for three min-utes without thinking about anything in particular. Should you think before you write? The answer is no! The correct order is for you to write before you think.

When in doubt, begin to write. It is not the quality of what to write, the fact that you write is most important. It should be stressed that the draft is very important to writing. Several drafts will be important before you reach your final product. Writing should be a journey of discovery, not just a demonstration of your thinking.

The process of responding to a piece of writing is a valuable skill to learn. The question to ask is "how does this sound?" It is important that the reader learns to build an internal response system. This response sys-tem should be directed to the writer's own writing and to the writing of others. In an initial response it should be non-evaluative. For a draft, always ask questions. Questions force writers to think and respond.

How do you teach the concept of revision? Revision is the same as re-seeing, re-thinking, and re-formulation. There should be a re-shaping of the writing and putting emphasis on re-constructing the original idea. The process of revision is similar to learning at a more penetrating level. The earliest stages of writing are the most important. Revision is the process of reaching completion and possible publication. Editors and proofreaders are experts at revision. Many children see this as the drudg-ery of writing but it is critical to teach the joy in thinking about learning at a more penetrating level and getting the sentence, the paragraph, and the total composition correct.

The process of evaluation is to teach the children how to critically look at their own work. Let the master question be, "What did I attempt to do in this paper?" Ask a series of other good questions that penetrate for sharper meaning. Ask them the question, "What could you do with this paper if you had another day?" An example of a critique is, "There are not enough examples to illustrate your key points." Also, "There is no valid conclusion and summary." After the child responds to these questions, tell him, "I have a surprise, you have another day."

It is ironic that students are asked to report conclusions in the writings but not to do the kind of writing to help them arrive at those excellent conclusions.

A big problem with writing, especially for the beginning writer, is that the writing is too superficial. The writing reveals nothing to the reader about what's on the writer's mind. There's generally an absence of thoughts presented. The senior year is the year of many college essays. Admission offices penetrate in their evaluation of the writing and find out that there's no thought behind it. This group holds in many cases an otherwise good application. There are specific activities that we can help our children arrive at conclusions and write prose that demonstrates a depth of thought.

Parents should be encouraged to initiate learning logs. This is the process of recording what the child thinks. Take a topic such as dinosaurs or African mammals, think about it and then write what you think.

While you, as a parent, are reading things around the kitchen table, in the car, or in the family room, ask what your children think about this particular writing. Ask what are the good and weak qualities of the writing. This can help to promote a constant evaluation of writing on the part of the child and will stimulate him to do better writing himself. Ask what he thinks of particular books. And keep track of the books he is reading in order to take every opportunity to discuss them and their contents. A healthy debate of the ideas found in the books read will stimulate a finer appreciation of good writing in others and stimulate good writing by the child. Keep track of old drafts for a comparison between early drafts and the final product. This shows the rapid improvement that can be made through the drafting process.

Encourage publication when your child writes something that shows great possibilities. Even weak writing that's published can lead to much better writing and future publishing dates. I encouraged publication for Mark and he published a book while he was in junior high. This book was mainly graphical, but the sense of accomplishment from this project has stayed with him to this day.

Develop research paper writing skills

Critical Issues List

How to do a research paper?

- *List subjects of interest*

- *Choose one for your paper*

- *Limit the topic*

- *Ask questions*

The first task for a research paper is to do some reading. This reading should take place over several days. Use several references. The second task is to list the questions that you have about the topic. The parents should sign off on the topics that are finally chosen.

If the topic, such as African civilizations, is chosen the following questions could be used," What is the nature of the various civilizations and cultures? Where was this culture and when was this culture? How do you describe the stages of this culture? For the artist in Africa, what was the media of choice?"

Another topic could be the linguistic connection of the people of Oceania and pre-Columbian America. The questions could include,

"What is the earliest known language of Oceania? Where was this language derived? When did writing as a language began? What is the earliest evidence to indicate the geographic spread of language? How does the local language absorb words of an imported language?" The next event is to narrow the topic with a question like, "What was the connection between the language of Oceania and Early American Indian languages?"

The next process is to revise the topic and questions. This is the single most important task. Have your child get a separate piece of paper for each question. At the top of the paper write one question. From now on in the research, only information on that question can be put on that paper.

Note sheets should be established. When collecting information, it is very important to distinguish between paraphrasing and plagiarism. Encyclopedias may not answer your questions directly. It is less necessary to go through the text of the articles and pick out the information related to your questions.

Make note sheets. This is a very important step. The child should learn the habit of taking good notes from materials he read because this will serve him well in future academic pursuits.

The writer must understand and avoid plagiarism. In order to do this, the child must distinguish between the summary, a paraphrase, and a direct quote. Give him one hour to do this exercise. But every piece of information that is written down must be identified in this manner. Summary should be followed by an "s," paraphrase should be followed by a "p," and a direct quote should be followed by the letters "dq." If your child hasn't done this, do not accept the note sheets.

The next step is to do research for a couple of weeks. Try to have five to ten minutes discussion everyday on the current topic. Take a notebook and jot down the points made in each discussion.

It is now time to write the report. Have the child put the note pages on a big table, and let him play around with the order. Develop an order which shows the introduction first, the body of the paper, and conclusions. Have your child take five minutes to write what was the most surprising thing about this topic. This can then be use for introduction of the topic and for summarizing the report.

The following approach is good writing technique to introduce your audience before you write. Imagine that there is someone who doesn't know anything about the topic. Putting that someone in mind helps to sharpen your understanding and clarify the expression of ideas.

Do activities with your children, like take a trip to the library to heighten interest in research. Watch educational videos, film strips, tapes, and listen to audio records.

Delay your thesis definition to the latest possible time in the writing process. Doing this early is generally too confining and narrows the scope of the writer. Have him read out loud the draft that he creates to see how it sounds. Mark experienced this system of writing as extra home work while studying in junior high.

Improve your mathematics skills

Mathematics has been considered by many to be the queen of the sciences. It is a language of logic that is simultaneously a product of thought and an instrument of thought. Math skills can carry over into many areas of academic pursuit. The sheer logic of it strengthens the mind's capacity to think and solve problems. Math was one of the early challenges we placed before Mark at an early age. We began with using computer games to stimulate his math interests. We rewarded his successes with little prizes. This helped to consolidate his mathematical way of thinking. As a parent, I felt that getting Mark ahead in math would serve several purposes. Math skills reflect greater thinking skills. Mathematics is objective and success with it is immediately understood. Confidence is built up quick. Test-taking skills are enhanced because all the important standard-ized tests have major math sections.

Our routine focused on helping Mark with the basic computational skills. One of his teachers established a program where the children were timed for completion of a sheet of math problems. The objective was to get everything correct in 1 minute. Mark's name was place on the bulletin board for having one of best records for these exercises. We set up pages of addition and subtraction problems. We timed him for one minute on each page. As he gained perfect marks on the pages, we made the problems pro-gressively more difficult. I typed up the multiplication tables and printed out all the numbers except the answers. He then worked on these until he had great proficiency in all the basic operations.

Around the seventh grade, we enrolled him briefly in a Kumon math program for a correspondence course. Although he worked with this program for only 5 months, we adapted several of their methods for Mark's benefit for the next few years. The Kumon math program was developed in 1954 by Mr. Toru Kumon. He developed this method while helping his own son gain proficiency in math. The level of math ranges from simple line drawing to university level mathematics. Students do repetitive worksheets on a daily basis until they reach 100% proficiency in a particular topic. There are well over 2 million children using this pro-gram around the world today. Several school districts in America have adopted this program as their choice for their mathematics program. While taking the program they generally get greatly improved grades in their math and in other courses because their skills improve and their atti-tude toward learning gets healthier. The essence of the program is to build the confidence of the child and establish a solid mathematical ability. The program builds success through:

1. The individual program:

The program develops a child not a class. The speed of progress is determined only by the child's rate of growth and the lessons are tailored for the individual.

2. Easy starting point:

Students are given a diagnostic test at the beginning. They begin at a level where they can be consistently proficient at 100%.

3. Developing good study habits:

Students are asked to set aside 10-to-30 minutes per day for the exercises of problem solving. They develop a joy for learning and become independent in their study. Habits are formed and the student sets more and more challenging goals.

4. Repetition of the work:

This is the key to the success of the program. Students have to repeat worksheets until they get 100% of the problems correct. The succeeding levels become easier because the students progress on the basis of strength.

5. Self-learning:

Students are taught to think and learn for themselves. There is minimal teacher intervention. The worksheets become the teacher. The student reads the problem and answers the questions alone. As the student reaches new material, he has the skill to conquer the unknown.

6. Good foundation for high school and college math:

The foundation is established for higher math. Students usually advance ahead of their grade level and begin high school math in primary school. By the time they reach high school, they are very familiar with the material.

The students usually go to a special center after regular school and pick up their worksheets. Students generally do 4 to 7 worksheets per day depending on the student's ability. Students are expected to get 100% correct and make corrections for all mistakes. They fill in scoring sheets which are reviewed by a supervisor.

We adopted some of these methods for Mark as he advanced in math. We acquired numerous workbooks on various levels of math. Mark always had two tracks of math work operating concurrently in his schedule. One track for regular school and another track for home exercises patterned after the Kumon method.

The other major push for math excellence occurred when Mark began preparing and taking the SAT in the seventh grade.

Learn from Bloom's taxonomy

The science of learning has been explained and classified by Bloom. Bloom's taxonomy is a classification system for learning.

The following are the 6 levels of Bloom's taxonomy:

- 1. Factual knowledge is the lowest level of learning.

- 2. Comprehension is the ability to grasp the meaning of material.

- 3. Application refers to the ability to use learned material in new and concrete situations.

- 4. Analysis is the ability to breakdown material into its component parts so that its organizational structure may be understood.

- 5. Synthesis refers to the ability to put parts together to form a new whole.

- 6. Evaluation is concerned with the ability to judge the value of material for a given purpose.

In Bloom's taxonomy 30 percent is fact, 30 percent is comprehension, 30 percent is application, and 10 percent is higher order thinking skill. Research indicates that many students focus 97 percent of the time on fact memorization. We need to spend more time on higher order thinking skills which involve analytical skills. Nearly 85 percent of facts are forgotten within three months. Learning has to go beyond mere facts. We need to create intellectual ambiguity because this stretches the child. Inform the child that not all problems have solutions—we sometimes need compromises. We should encourage a bright child to give commitment to complete a project, particularly an ambiguous, challenging problem.

Most textbooks are written in Bloom's taxonomy level one. "We must guide our craft by the stars and not by the light of the passing ship," Bradley said. We have to convert Bloom's taxonomy level one into all of Bloom's taxonomy. We have to teach tolerance for ambiguity. When your child answers a question, the defense of the answer is more important than whether the answer is correct or not.

Learn Test-taking Skills

"What shall we do when hope is gone?" The words leapt out like a leaping sword. 'Sail on! Sail! Sail! And on!"

—*Anonymous*

"If I hear, I forget; if I see, I remember; if I do , I make it my own."

—*Chinese saying*

Start early

Mark began taking the Stanford Early School Achievement test in first grade. In the skills analysis section, Mark's achievements in sounds and letters were in the intermediate percentiles; his achievements in word reading was in the 90 plus percentile; incentives reading was in the 95 percentile; listening was in the 70 percentile; mathematics was in the 95 percentile; environment was in the 95 percentile; reading was in the 90 percentile; and total reading was in the 90 plus percentile. He was rated above average in 15 skill categories. He improved every year he took this test. And by the third grade, this confidence in skill in Test-taking had reached the level where he was above average in all the test areas. In six of the categories he was in the 99th percentile. We used these tests to judge Mark's progress in the International School. This was possible because children across America take this test and the scores achieved are always comparable to that of students in the United States. We judged the quality of his education by the high scores that Mark consistently received on these tests, from first grade throughout his elementary school years.

Talented and gifted programs and the SAT-I/Try progressively more difficult tests

There are several programs in United States that have been designed to tap talented youth. The most famous of the programs and one of the pioneers is the Center for Talented Youth (CTY) program at Johns Hopkins University. In 1971, Dr. Julian Stanley founded a study of mathematically precocious youth. This program has grown into a very expansive program covering many disciplines for youth all over the world. The key program is called Talent Search: Seventh Grade Academic Programs. This program was started in 1980. It requires students in the seventh grade to take the SAT and qualify with a score of at least 500 on the math and at least 930 for the verbal and math combined. They now also have talent searches of the fifth and six grades and also there's a program for those in grades three through seven.

The main program has identified more than 425,000 students. In 1994 over 38,000 seventh grade students took the SAT exam. The students who are accepted into the program participate in research and the results add to our understanding of cognitive development and high-level achievement. The classes are usually designed to provide the total immersion experience in one subject. For example, those taking calculus at the seventh grade level will finish the course in three weeks. They generally spend eight hours per day studying the subject. It is very intense but the outcome is very rewarding for the students.

The students benefit in many ways in the program. They benefit from engaging and rigorous academic work along with a very talented peer group. This peer group has a tremendous positive impact on the students. They learn what their strengths and weaknesses are in a given subject area. They also learn better and effective discipline and study habits. The students are generally in class for five hours per day, and after class they have regular study hours established.

A similar program was established at Northwestern University in 1982. They have an annual academic talent search across the country. The center works with educators and school districts to develop services for gifted students. They provide workshops and access to resources for parents and students. The summer program is for students to develop as talented adolescents. The students study with strong teachers and have an intellectual interaction with a peer group that is extraordinary. They take one intensive fast pace course during the three-week period. Classes meet for five hours per day for five days a week and extensive homework is required for many courses. In the math classes, exams are given at the end of the chapter. Students are not allowed to proceed until they pass satisfactorily the exams on each topic. It is a grueling and intensive experience. For the mathematics program for the seventh grade, a SAT-I score of 520 is required on the math and 920 on the math and verbal combined.

The benefits of the Northwestern program are similar to those of the students of the Johns Hopkins program. Mark was accepted in the Northwestern program but he did not attend because he decided to go to the Philips Exeter summer program that summer. His brother Geoffrey later attended that program with great success. How did they prepare for acceptance in this program?

Once we heard about the program, I showed Mark brochures and information. We discussed the programs, their goals, and objectives. I later asked whether he would be interested in trying to qualify for this program. He said he wanted to think about it. He took the brochures and read them on his own without pressure from his parents. He later came back to tell us he would like to give it a try. So we began the odyssey of intensive preparation.

The Sat-I

The testing is a very important part of the application process. This is unfortunate because there are scholars who think that the test does not measure unbiased intelligence or potential. Colleges, however, make judgments about students based on this test and it's important to do well. How do you prepare for the test? It is recommended that students begin taking the SAT-I when they're in the seventh grade. Why take the test this early? The most important reason for taking the test early is to establish a high standard in the mind of the student. The test is clearly over his head at that age but it stretches his thinking and lets him know what the test is all about. It doesn't matter whether the score is in the low 300's or middle 400's; the important thing is for the student to begin to realize the challenges ahead in academic life. Therefore, if the student is really prepared for this exam and scored above 500 in the math and verbal sections, he can qualify for several unique summer programs for high-school students at the seventh grade level in various colleges. Students from around the country can participate in these programs after reaching cut-off scores in the mid-500's.

The results of the math and verbal sections can point out areas of weakness. They can generate a diagnosis that tells a student the areas where he has strengths and the areas where he has weaknesses. It can also stimulate a wider reading interest which is the best preparation in the long run for SAT testing. Mark was very enthusiastic about taking his first test. All the other students were much older. He sat with them for the full three hours, working hard on all the questions that he knew and skipping those he did not. When he got his results back, he was not quite disappointed but clearly happy that he had taken the test. He did not qualify for the Center for Talent Development Program that time, but he was well on his way because he was prepared and looked forward to taking the exam again.

When Mark began taking the SAT in the sixth grade, the score barely reached 400 in the verbal and math portions. In spite of that apparent failure, taking the exam was really a big success. He had the chance to sit in the exam hall with older students, he had the chance to exercise his mental capacities with difficult material, and he gained the confidence of having to sit through the exam the first time. On subsequent occasions, this performance rapidly improved. We worked with a math tutor to help him prepare for the test. This proved to be invaluable because the math teacher demonstrated many shortcuts and went through many problems on the sample test to familiarize Mark with all of the major types of problems. Significant portions of the sample test were related to subjects he had not taken before, and he had to become familiar with the subjects in order to reasonably manage the test. Although his results were very low in the beginning, Mark was happy to get these results.

After two years and a half years of taking this test on a periodic basis, improvement was beginning to show. This improvement in our view was more rapid than one might expect. This proved in Mark's mind that he was doing better on a difficult assignment, and he had a sense of clearly doing a good job. This was, of course, one of the most important reason for taking the exam early in the first place.

By the time he reached the eighth grade, he scored over 550 on the math and a collective 930 on the math and verbal. This qualified him for the Center for Talent Development program at Northwestern University. When that occurred, he saw the impact of long, hard work which resulted in this achievement. His math teacher, was notably proud and began telling Mark that he would later qualify for MIT.

Excellence is Worth the Cost

"Too many develop every talent except the talent to use all other talents—will power."

"The best preparation for tomorrow is to do today's work supremely well."

—Anonymous

Critical Issues List

Indicators of excellence

- *Make a commitment to a given activity or project*
- *Excellence in academics is expected*
- *Seek to demonstrate excellence outside of academics*
- *Show evidence of progress and development*
- *Demonstrate recognition for your excellence*

What do colleges look for that distinguish you from other applicants? Excellence ranks high on the list. What is excellence? Remember all applicants applying to select colleges show high levels of achievement. It is your responsibility to compete by demonstrating a level of excellence which is above and beyond the average. Your application has to standout in the crowd.

Excellence is demonstrated through several key factors. One factor is commitment to a given activity or project. Mark demonstrated this through his commitment over several years to the Boy Scouts program.

He achieved the rank of Eagle Scout, which is the highest possible indicator of excellence that the program can measure.

Green and Minton described what they call the spiritual qualities of excellence. They suggest that it is a spiritual quality toward the attitude of excellence and that one must listen to their inner voice which inspires them to achieve at their highest capability.

Excellence in academics is expected. Therefore, seek to demonstrate excellence outside of academics, in fields like athletics and arts. It is there that you must show your talent. According to Green and Minton, the selective colleges look for three essential characteristics of excellence in non-academic areas. The first is commitment. Colleges want to see that you have committed yourself to an activity, and this is judged through the number of years that you have spent working several hours per day in this activity. The more intense the involvement and the commitment, the more respect that the admission counselors will render. When a student has devoted 10 hours per week on average for the last seven years to an activity, that brings respect. Mark swam during swim season for this stretch of time over several years. Inevitably, much discipline develops from this type of commitment. We saw that in Mark as he grew to love his sport, and he never complained about the time he devoted to perfecting his craft.

The next characteristic that is expected is evidence of development. If you have spent time in special summer programs to develop your skills, make that known to the committee. Also show the growth and improvement achieved over the years, through better competition times and the winning of medals. Of all of things that admissions offices enjoy, they like to see a candidate who has shown growth and improvement in whatever he has attempted and pursued over the years. They can forgive poor performances in early years, but they will look for command performances in the later year. Show this in your documentation. Show them that you have done something, show them where you have learned a tangible skill and perfected it. If you spot an organization in your school such as a chess club or environmental group, show how the organization expanded its group of activities. Show how you took a job in an office supply store and how you progressed from stocking clerk to assistant manager in a short time. Show your motivation to advance yourself.

The next component of excellence that should be demonstrated is recognition. The admission committees especially value newspaper articles about your accomplishments. An award that you have received for your volunteer work indicates that other people recognize and appreciate your contribution. Sometimes this may mean that you must contact your local newspaper to get the story told. This is not glorious publicity seeking but is very practical for establishing a paper trail of your accomplishments. Letters from people who work with you on every project or your supervisor are particularly helpful for the committees. These are not considered the same as teachers' recommendations but are considered items which amplify things about your work and your personality that are not found in the rest of your application. You don't need to send all certificates or evidence of your achievements. A few of these items sprinkled in with your application in a special exhibit section could be very helpful.

The concept of flow

Perhaps the most powerful tool in achieving excellence in any endeavor is the ability to reach a state of flow. Mihaly Csikszentmihalyi of the University of Chicago defines flow as an optimal experience which stretches a person's capacity and involves the element of novelty and risk. When things are going well the state of consciousness has been described as effortless, highly focused, and automatic. Most striking, a very wide spectrum of performers describe flow in the same way. That includes scientists, artists, sports performers, and writers.

A prerequisite for flow to function is the necessity to have many hours of practice in the activity being pursued. With practice the neural circuits are well developed and hard-wired. Flow occurs when the performer is in a relaxed mental state and reaches peak performance. This is a mental zone where excellence and great performance come easily and almost effortlessly while the mind focuses almost exclusively on the activity while blotting out the world.

Flow is probably the most effective means of teaching a child anything. The positive energy and pleasurable sensations a child gets from achieving excellence through flow is self-sustaining. Being attracted to the mental pleasure that is achieved through flow, the child is internally motivated to return time and time again. Practice becomes pleasure rather than drudgery.

A study was done at a magnet school for math and sciences in Chicago. Students were rated as high achievers or low achievers among their group. Both, however, scored better than the 95th percentile in math. They were all given beepers and at random times they were beeped. When the beeper sounded the students recorded what they were doing and what the mood was. The high achievers spent their time studying because it was a pleasing experience, for 40% of the time. On the other hand, the low achievers only achieved flow while studying 16% of the time. The low achievers found more flow and pleasure while socializing than while studying.

This study's results suggest that achievement can be enhanced through teaching flow and helping a child develop internal energy and motivation toward excellence.

According to the research of Csikszentmihalyi, there are nine main elements described by those who are creative and reach flow: *"1) there are clear goals every step of the way; 2) there is immediate feedback to one's actions; 3) there is a balance between challenges and skills; 4) action and awareness are merged; 5) distractions are excluded from consciousness; 6) there is no worry of failure; 7) self-consciousness disappears; 8) the sense of time becomes distorted; and 9) the activity becomes autoletic."*

Csikszentmihalyi talks further about the evolution of consciousness and flow. The typical things that give us pleasure such as sex, power, fame and material things are well established in our genetic makeup. Seeking these things have been tied to survival and many of these things are thousands of years old. Those things that are relatively recent in evolution such as manipulating abstract symbols to create in science, math, and language are more difficult to associate with pleasure. Creative individuals achieve something special through flow. They achieve pleasure and happiness in activities that many people find difficult and frustrating. The world is much better off having these individuals around. The educational system for our children needs to establish a method which helps large numbers of individuals to find pleasure in creative activities in the world of sports, music, literature, and science.

Establish a track record of excellence

Mark established a particularly strong track record of excellence through his efforts in several extracurricular activities. One activity that involved tremendous amounts of work and investments of time was scouting. Swimming was another activity that also required a sustained commitment and great amounts of physical work. Music was the third activity that Mark spent many years gaining proficiency in. In these activities Mark worked diligently to establish a track record of excellence.

Scouting

Critical Issues List

- *Critical issues*

- *Socialization*

- *Planning, developing, and implementing projects*

- *Advancement*

- *Arrow of Light and Eagle Scout*

We took Mark to his first Cub Scout meeting when he was in the second grade. This meeting began a long process of involvement in the scouting movement that gave tremendous benefits to Mark. Our initial thoughts for involving Mark in the Boy Scouts were to have him do many things collectively. The first idea was socialization. As a non-school activity, Mark could make friends with other boys and learn how to communicate and work with others. In life, it is very important to perfect this skill of getting along with others. In school and in the future workplace, being able to get along with others establishes your position in organizations and in groups of people. The second idea was for Mark to participate in planning, developing, and implementing projects. He would start in the Cub Scouts with small projects and advance in the Boy Scouts to large-scale projects. The third idea was to have Mark participate in an activity where he could have fun and go on trips, especially camping trips. Mark realized all of these goals in his scouting experience, and this began with the Cub Scouts.

Generally speaking, on one night of the week, we took Mark to den meetings. Sometimes he would go straight from school by bus to the den meetings. The scout activities in the beginning were very simple and basic, but they established a discipline for Mark to attend meetings, to work with others and plan activities as a group. He was very happy and enjoyed working with other scouts. And we took the same philosophy that we took from any other activity, that having fun was the chief reason and the highest priority. One thing he began to learn was goal setting. In the Cub Scouts when productivity produces results, there is a reward of a new badge and eventually a new rank. There was a constant anticipation of what could be accomplished in this organization and developing productive activity to reach a given goal. He slowly began to progress in the ranks of the cub scouts, and for each level of advancement there was a ceremonial occasion. On these occasions, he could see what the other boys were accomplishing, and he could also reap the reward of this hard work. Eventually, he reached the highest level of the cub scouts by earning the Arrow of Light. This was very important for Mark to attain this. As parents, we realized that you cannot underestimate the psychology of these award ceremonies and the reinforcing power that they have for the child's self-esteem. Once Mark received the Arrow of Light award, he then began to look for new worlds to conquer. The next step was to begin Boy Scouts.

Mark's experience in the Cub Scouts prepared him for the challenge ahead in the Boy Scouts. Going to meetings was now a routine. However, he had to start again, as a Tenderfoot. There were many ranks ahead to get promoted to and the ultimate challenge of the Eagle Scout award loomed in the distant horizon. This long-term goal setting, I think, is one of the strong advantages of Boy Scouts. I consistently told Mark about the difficulty of achieving Eagle Scout but at the same time I told him that he could do it. I believed this helped him to have more determination to pursue the goal of Eagle Scout and helped him to achieve the ability to reach that goal. I have also applied this strategy to other areas of activity, including sports and music. By him having this long-term goal and reinforcing that in his mind, he had the ability to stick to the task. One of the greatest problems of the scouts is the drop out rate. Many boys join but drop out after a few months or after a few years. I think that the greatest reason for the high drop out rate is that many of the boys do not firmly fix their mind on a long-term goal. With a long-term goal firmly in their thoughts, it is much more difficult to drop out. Even if scouting becomes boring or becomes too difficult, the scout is more likely to stick to the task and persevere. Although Mark was at a young age, I think one of the most valuable lessons he learned from scouting was perseverance.

The pace of scouting and its activities took the skills acquisition to a higher level. Generally, Mark went to scout meetings on Saturday evenings after school. The meetings lasted from 7:00 to 9:30 p.m. During that time, Mark was active in meetings, planning activities, being tested for merit badge proficiency, and making new friends. This level of intense activity took place over several years, while Mark consistently made progress which reinforced his loyalty to the scout movement. The older boys and the leaders provided solid role models for Mark. Because this particular scout troop was in a foreign country, there was a lot of turnover in boys who were members and in the adult leadership. We were fortunate to have a vibrant movement that provided this outlet for the boys. The U.S. military presence in Saudi Arabia was the solid foundation for the support of an organization of the scouting movement. For those who do not have knowledge of the scouts in your area, a good place to start your search would be at the local churches. This has been a natural base of many scout programs around the country. Even if you have to drive a distance to get your son or daughter to a scout troop, make the sacrifice to get them there. I found over the years that although my evening was taken almost completely by scouting, the benefits to Mark over the years were more than worth the sacrifice.

Scouting provided Mark with a new peer group. This was a group with a certain set of interests and a group who also shared in the same long-term goal. I think that another important advantage of scouting was the maturing experience it provided. The teamwork activities taught Mark at another level how to deal with others and work well with others. I'm sure that there were many skills that he gained from this experience which he has applied to other situations.

One of the important activities in scouting was camping. Typically, camp outs would require several weeks of preparation for the boys. They were organized by patrol groups. The scouts had to make a list of all of the items they needed for camp and they had to organize the different tasks required for camping such as cooking and washing. Scouts were designated to carry out certain activities and be responsible for specific tasks. Many times, Mark had to go to the supermarket to shop for the essential food items needed for the camp outs. This entire process taught him the skills of responsibility, loyalty to the group, and a sense of shared accomplishment. Most importantly, the boys had a lot of fun. The benefits of living near Riyadh offered many sites for exciting, scenic, rough, and challenging camping excursions.

A particularly difficult challenge in scouting was the completion of merit badge requirements. In many areas such as biology, communication, electronics, community service, citizenship, and environment, Mark had to gain extra knowledge in order to pass oral and sometimes written tests. These were important benchmarks and milestones toward advancement through the ranks. After completing the required number of merit badges, the scout was then qualified to take a test before a review board to pass from one rank to another. The ranks included ,Tenderfoot, Second-class, First-class, Star, Life and ultimately the Eagle rank. Again, as in the Cub Scouts, each rank resulted in a ceremonial occasion. These were great times for the boys to organize a ceremony and to be awarded merit badges and new ranks that they deserved from their efforts. It was always a positive reinforcing experience, and clearly rewards and awards are the fuel which keep the productive scout going.

Although many of Marks friends who initially joined scouting with him had dropped out, Mark never once suggested that he quit. He resisted quitting because he firmly established a long-term goal and stuck to it.

Music

We started Mark with music very early. We began by playing music around the house while he was an infant and a young child. Because of our personal taste in music, he mostly heard jazz and some classical music. I had read that plants even grew better when they were surrounded by greatly composed music. Also, much research has demonstrated the benefits of music to children.

In my discussion with musicians, it was clear that learning the piano should be the first step in a musical career. We were fortunate to find a piano teacher in Riyadh. At the same time I bought an instrument which was an electronic piano. We began our weekly trips to the piano teacher. Mark rapidly progressed in learning to play the piano and read music with an excellent teacher. He continued this practice for over a year. During that time, he gave several recitals and had a weekly and daily schedule of practicing at home. This routine of practice further gave him the discipline to focus on a given task at hand. I could see that he was beginning to enjoy his music. Although it took several months of challenge for him to get real enjoyment from practice, slowly over time, he would volunteer to go on his own without being asked.

In the fifth grade in his school, Mark was asked to join the school band. This was usually reserved for students who had high academic grades and who showed an interest in performing music. Mark was assigned a trumpet. In this grade he had music assigned as a regular class session, for five times a week. The experience he had gained from the piano served him well, and he was able to make the transition to a new instrument very smoothly.

The band program at the International School was a well-organized, very effective program with excellent teachers. Mark learned to read more advanced music and his joy of music increased. He enjoyed the trumpet at first, but later switched to the baritone because the band needed players of that instrument. It is well established that the child who plays an instrument is the child who learns to listen. Listening is a very important skill in the arts and in academia.

As parents, we enjoyed music that Mark played because we knew that he would develop a lifelong habit and skill. This habit would enhance his appreciation of life. We also enjoyed the concerts that were periodically performed by his school band. Three to four times per year, the band had concert performances, and parents and the community turned out in large numbers to hear the new songs learned by the students. Many parents took the opportunity to videotape their students performing. We also found that the peer groups in music were academically inclined and were a very positive influence on each other.

Playing in the band at school gave Mark a sense of accomplishment and enhanced his self-esteem. A competition was held on a yearly basis for selection to be a member of the country-wide band. Mark entered and won this competition to participate in a concert with musicians from other parts of Saudi Arabia. This band had a guest conductor, and this was a remarkable experience in learning new songs quickly and performing them before a large audience. There was the risk of failure when entering a competition (more in section on risk taking). We stressed that this type of risk is okay and failure is not particularly a bad thing. Indeed, it is a positive reinforcement for motivation to succeed in the future.

There is an advantage of taking your child to many new activities to explore their potential. Many talents, unfortunately, go hidden for a lifetime. It is our responsibility as parents to help the child dabble and experiment with new activities. Intrinsic to this process is the possibility that you'll discover a hidden talent in your child. Many great artists were discovered through the activities of the parents in providing the opportunity for the children to explore, expand, and develop new things. We never dreamed that Mark would pursue concert music as a career. If he had chosen this or his talents allowed him to be so, then okay. Our main objective as parents was not to push such a career, but to enhance his appreciation of music and of life. I think we accomplished this task. He continued to play the baritone in bands and orchestras through the completion of high school.

This helps the college application process when a student has to list his extracurricular activities. The process of devoting long hours to music or the course of development pays off, by providing a child with new skills and abilities. There is also research evidence that show enhancement of brain development. Studies have shown that students who learned music also do better in math than a control group. This is related to the connection of neurons in the brain. When an activity becomes a habit, the neurons become hard wired in certain pathways. The same pathway that influences ability in math also influences the ability in music.

Although we had to buy several different instruments at various times, we found that this investment paid off in unseen ways. Most importantly, Mark began to enjoy playing music and to show a great appreciation for music.

Physical exercise and sports

Sports are very important in the development of the child. The most important thing that a sport accomplishes is to establish a disciplined balance to academics. An academically rigorous regime requires its opposite, namely, sports and physical activity. Having regular physical activity establishes discipline for the child. Perhaps most importantly, the health of the child is optimized through the regular exposure to physical exercise. We always took Mark out to run and play, from the time he began to walk. We focused on one sport for Mark. If the child is athletically gifted it is important to explore several sports to find out where his exceptional talents are. If the facilities are available the exploration of golf and tennis at an early age could yield enormous rewards down the road if the child shows great potential. Tiger Woods and Pete Sampras are examples of the potential in these sports. The major sports of basketball, football and baseball are also very popular and are worth the experience. Regardless of the objective or the motivation behind the exploration of a sport, there are great health benefits to physical activity and exercise. If a child starts at an early age they have the chance to develop real solid skills and expertise in a sport. This skill could be very useful at the time of college admissions if the level achieved by them is seen as an asset to the college athletic program. A goal of excellence is a worthy goal in any sports for multiple reasons.

As Mark grew older, we found, through experience and investigation, that swimming was an excellent sport for children and adults. We consequently focused our efforts on improving Mark's swimming ability. I taught him how to swim at the very young age of three or four years. Whenever we had the chance, I took him to a pool and spent time playing around and combining that with lessons on how to swim. When he was approximately seven years of age, he began to take training sessions for a future in competitive swimming. The exercise generally lasted half an hour and revolved around doing laps and learning proper stroke technique in the pool. After he began this regular routine of swimming, we noticed that his sleeping improved tremendously.

At first, he complained about the hard work involved and the general difficulty found in swimming laps. I told him to continue with the workouts for a short while in order to decide whether to continue or quit swimming. It was an ongoing debate for many months. Gradually I saw his attitude change, and he grew to love the sport in which he was quickly gaining proficiency. We were rapidly reaching the critical time that I think all parents should strive to reach with their children. That time is when a difficult rigorous sport or activity transforms itself into an enjoyable fun activity. This happened for Mark in swimming. The priority for this activity always was to have fun. As Mark began to enjoy swimming, we decided to shift into a competitive age group swimming program. In that program he met children his age who were actively training and competing in swim meets, for constant improvement in their times. His stroke technique, endurance, and all-around stamina eventually improved dramatically. Swim competitions for Mark took approximately half a day during week-ends. At these competitions families used to join their children and run the meets. This advanced the bond between parents and children. Although swimming took up considerable time in training, we found that Mark's grades always improved during training periods. I used to tell him that swimming caused more blood circulation to the brain and therefore he could be smarter. His self-esteem grew rapidly under the swimming regime. He never complained anymore and as he grew older he grew stronger, more confident and healthier with this sport that he could call his own.

Mark grew to love the sports of swimming. He would volunteer to go train, even when the team was not training. At the time of competition, he prepared himself psychologically and physically for the races. In the course of participating in hundreds of swim meets and competing on such a reg-ular basis and relying on all the skills to win, the competitive instincts for Mark were sharpened. This made Mark more competitive in activities that he has participated in, including academic. Although it was nice to win, we always stressed to Mark that his goal in any race was to swim his per-sonal best time. Losing was not a bad thing, we only stressed for him to make a personal best time. Even in academic performance, the main con-cern was not how Mark ranked with other students but how he ranked against himself on previous exams. The yardstick was whether there was improvement in his performance based on his best efforts. This removed the unnecessary stress that winning always puts on a child.

It doesn't matter what sport the child participates in. It is important to make sure that your child is in a sport that can build health, confidence, and self-esteem. We chose swimming because it is generally injury free. Many sports are plagued by serious and sometimes life-threatening injuries. It is not a sport that can make you suddenly rich after you turn professional. The benefits far outweigh the disadvantages, however. We notice that children who swam generally had high academic achievement and also played music. Other sports also exhibit this benefit. We therefore felt that through school, college and university that the friends Mark would make would be an excellent group to be a part of. While in grade school, junior high and high school the swim group was an excellent influence on Mark.

Swimming is renowned for training all muscle groups. There is very much research evidence to show its health benefits. When you're swimming it is a relatively gravity-free sport. There are generally less injuries involved in swimming. It has the unique quality of being a team sport like basketball and an individual sport like gymnastics. It helps provide discipline for the child in the individual endeavor and challenges, and it provides experience in teamwork and cooperation with others. Once the child hits the water, what happens between the walls of the pool is determined by the actions of the swimmer alone. There are individual races, and there are group races call relays. Another feature of swimming is the ability to swim for exercise until old age. This makes the benefits a lifelong advantage.

When Mark left home for boarding school, he immediately made contact with the swimming program at Phillips Academy. He found that the hard work and training that he had accomplished over the past seven years paid off handsomely. He made the cut for the swim team while those without previous experience failed. This gave him a sense of accomplishment at his new school and built his self-esteem to a new level. I think he really began to appreciate the hard work that he had invested in swimming. Clearly, the comparison to other areas of activity is valid. When one invests his time and effort and worked over long periods with a particular activity the big payoff in dividends of achievement are down the road. During the high school swim season, Mark's swimming improved tremendously and he was able to earn a varsity letter in the sport. This experience helped him adapt to the rigorous academic program of the school and gave him a sense of belonging to a leading school. Most importantly, he developed the school spirit and the sense of dedication and responsibility to the work of the team while swimming during that first year. He subsequently swam during the three years at Phillips Academy and later joined the varsity at MIT, in Cambridge.

Tutors and Summer Programs

"Learn all you can from others. The school of experience takes so long that the graduates are too old to go to work."

—Henry Ford

Tutors can strengthen weaknesses

We found out as parents that we could not teach everything to our child. We found a music teacher to teach music, we found swim coaches to coach swimming, and later found a math teacher to teach math. Most parents think that it's okay to get a tutor for music, but they do not stretch and think that an extra teacher can be useful for academic subjects. In this key area, most people assume that children get enough from their teachers and school. This is clearly not true in most schools. Even in the International School, parents readily campaign to the school board about children having too much homework. On the contrary, there was a need, in my opinion, for extra input. The logic that parents used to argue against homework was "let my child enjoy his childhood." They imply through this expression that homework destroys the childhood. A child has ample time to have fun and enjoy himself along with learning and to appreciate the joy of learning.

I found a math tutor quite by accident. I met a friend and mentioned the problem of math instruction and asked him whether he knows of anyone who could teach math in his spare time. Within a few days my friend called back and explained that he had a friend, a math teacher, who agreed to help out. We contacted this teacher, visited his house, and this began an eight-year relationship that was extraordinarily beneficial for Mark.

From this experience, I learned, as a parent, that academic tutors are useful and very valuable for giving a child an edge in the academic competition. The first task for the tutor was to prepare Mark for the Scholastic Aptitude Test (SAT) exam, even though he was only in the sixth grade. He began by going over the mistakes that Mark made on a practice SAT exam and showing him techniques for solving the problems. The tutor engineered Mark's understanding in a reverse manner by taking the problem and explaining the method and then going back to the principles which led to this type of problem. This may fly in the face of conventional educational wisdom but Mark found it helpful. The most important thing preparing for this SAT test was to introduce the excitement of a new journey. Mark's weakness and strengths were readily identified through the test. He began to grasp ideas and concepts in math that were several years ahead, and the math he studied in school became more understandable and easier. Mark progressed, by taking the understanding of math through a problem-by-problem approach, furthermore he had fun learning.

If your child is weak in any subject area in school, find someone who can spend an extra two or three hours per week with him to teach the essence of the subject matter. Also, if you would like your child to move ahead of the material he is presently studying, find a tutor who can introduce him to advanced material. Develop goals around the material and work toward that goal step-by-step.

The first step to begin looking for a tutor is to ask around in your town or community. The best place is the school your child attends. Many teachers in the regular schools also have extra jobs tutoring in the afternoon and evening. When the tutoring becomes a routine, your child will find school more interesting and easy. Parents will be very pleased to see the grades improve for their children. The variation of this idea is standard practice in many developing countries of the world. Parents, who want to see their children get ahead and have a better life, sacrifice to find a second school after regular school. This occurs in countries that include Japan, Turkey, Egypt, India, Taiwan, and European countries like Germany.

There are some programs like the Sylvan Learning Centers that have cropped up around the U.S. that point to the future. Some school districts have contracted with Sylvan Learning Centers to help their students improve reading and mathematics skills. The trend is for parents to seek extra academic support for their children in a weak public school system. The competition for selective colleges is becoming keener and parents want to have their children prepare for this challenge.

The teacher will teach his wisdom, discipline, and perspective to the child as a significant byproduct of coaching and tutoring. This go beyond the subject matter covered, the music, or the sport played. This may be a fresh perspective slightly different from what the parent teaches and opens the child to a broader view. The challenge and advantage the child gets are to learn from many teachers, rather than just parents and the teachers in school. We found that Mark learned more discipline from his tutor than from his regular teachers.

Try summer programs

Mark participated in a critical summer program between eighth grade year and his ninth grade year. He applied and was accepted to a program at Phillips Exeter Summer School and a talented and gifted program at Northwestern University. These were two very good programs, and the Northwestern program required that he qualify by getting a specific score on the SAT exam. Mark decided to go to the 6-week Exeter program in order to take several courses instead of the one allowed at the 3-week

Northwestern program. This experience provided him with the first chance to go away from home on his own. It was a great learning experience, and he was able to adapt to a large campus and a rigorous academic environment. He studied mathematics where he received honors, expository writing, swimming, and water polo. He made many friends and learned the rudiments of budgeting his money and handling his own affairs. Summer programs offer full immersion in a new environment and in a relatively short time period.

For a complete guide to summer programs use *Peterson's Guide to Summer Programs.*

Part III

The College Application Process

Admission Principles

"Writing down your six most urgent tasks for tomorrow develops judgment, memory, imagination, and efficiency."

"There's a proper place for everyone. But it won't search for us. We must search for it."

"Enthusiasm is the invisible magnet that draws others to our view."

—Anonymous

This is a quote from MIT's viewbook.

"What does it take to get into MIT?"

"MIT's admissions decisions are based on evaluations of applications by members of the admission staff, faculty members, and an admissions committee. Evaluations focus on candidates' grades, the quality of their academic program, standardized test scores, personal accomplishments, and such characteristics as creativity, leadership, and love of learning."

Critical Issues List

There are several important issues that must be addressed in the college application process.

- *Testing*

- *The application*

- *Recommendations*

- *Transcript grades*

- *Interview*

- *Supplemental materials*

- *Financial aid*

- *Athletes and recruitment*

Establish an admissions calendar

A student should carefully prepare a calendar that will cover the months of his junior and senior years during the college admissions process. The long-term calendar should begin in elementary school with a focus on the years leading up to high school graduation. This calendar should establish all the deadlines for critical events during this period. When the child has prepared himself over the years for the grueling test of college admissions, it is important to follow through at this level with great care. Why prepare all of the years before and put forth so much effort in so many areas of endeavor and fail with the application process? The application should be filled out with great care. All parts should be completed neatly and preferably typed. There are new computer programs available that permit a student to fill the application completely by computer. Also many colleges use the common application which permits a student to fill out one application for numerous colleges. Read all the instructions very carefully and follow them to the letter. Make sure all deadlines are met. It is suggested that you make a copy of all applications and practice filling them out before your final draft. Make corrections of the applications that you fill out and create a separate file folder for each school.

Admissions Calendar

Elementary School
> *Develop the habits necessary for excellence*
> *Learn to enjoy school*
> *Learn how to study and achieve high grades*
> *Start extracurricular activities and sports you enjoy*

Middle School
> *Begin to visit colleges*
> *Try to qualify for talented and gifted programs (take SAT-I)*
> *Maintain a strong transcript*

High School

Ninth grade
> *Plan your courses for the entire 4 years*
> *Develop strong extracurricular interests*
> *Strive for strong grades*

Tenth grade
> *Continue taking the SAT-I test*
> *Strengthen commitment to various extracurriculars*
> *Concentrate on one or two sports*
> *Take challenging courses (AP when possible) and get excellent grades*

Eleventh grade
> *Take PSAT*
> *Establish rapport with your college counselor and develop a list of colleges*
> *Take SAT-I*
> *Continue with challenging courses (AP when possible)and excellent grades*
> *Excel in your extracurricular activities (have fun)*

Summer between Junior and Senior year
    Visit colleges on your list
    Begin your college applications and the essays

Senior Year
    Prepare your applications meticulously
    Take the SAT-I test again if necessary
    Take honors or AP courses where possible
    Get applications in mail for Early Decision or Regular pool
    Make decision on acceptances

Prepare far ahead for each requirement

Stanford University's criteria for admission as stated in their publications.

"The primary criterion for admission is academic excellence, and the most important single credential is the transcript. There are no minimum figures set for grade point average, test scores, or rank in class, nor are there specific high school course requirements for entrance to Stanford. We do, however, require evidence of successful completion of an accredited secondary school program, and we look for those students who have selected as rigorous an academic program as possible, and who have achieved distinction in a range of academic courses. Our ablest candidates have mostly "A"s in their courses, but we do find that some students with lower grade averages may show more real promise for strong college-level course work than some students with higher averages. We find the same may apply with regard to test scores—very high scores, though they may in many cases confirm scholastic promise, do not guarantee admission to Stanford. It is always to an applicant's benefit to have taken the most demanding courses available in high school. A strong performance in accelerated, honors, or Advanced Placement classes indicates a student's ability and desire to meet academic challenges."

The following is recommended as basic preparation for study at Princeton:

- four years of English (including continued practice in writing)

- four years of mathematics

- four years of one foreign language

- at least two years of laboratory science

- at least two years of history (including that of a country or an area outside the United States)

- some study of art, music, and, if possible, a second foreign language

Focus on selective colleges

Critical Issues List

Admission groups

- *Intellects*

- *Special talent*

- *Family legacy group*

- *Social conscience group*

- *Well-rounded student*

It is important for candidates to understand that colleges cannot look at the entire class as one group to take their selections for the upcoming class. The colleges admissions committees divide the class into several groups to make the selections. Applicants who fall within various categories are generally competing among themselves, and not with other members of the class. Understanding this concept helps candidates prepare for the grueling admission process by positioning themselves for being competitive in one or more of these special groups. One of the best categorization rendered is one developed by Richard Moll, a former admissions officer at several colleges.

This first group are the intellects. The most selective colleges want a group of academically oriented students who have distinguished themselves in various academic fields. These are students who have taken the top course loads and have produced stellar performances in all the academic pursuits. They are the academic jocks, if you will. Furthermore, they have also performed in the upper one percent of the United States in · testing, scoring 1550's on the SAT-I and the 750's on the SAT-II exams. They bring a level of academic capabilities that challenge the teachers and raise the level of the entire institution. They are very important for the reputation of the college as an academic powerhouse and they liven the discussions in the classroom. If you have excelled academically and can perform at these levels, you have a very high percentage chance of being admitted to the most selective colleges. In MIT, the Ivy League, and the other top schools, this is only 1/4 or 1/5 of the admitted class. Most applicants are competing against applicants in other pools, rather than this intellectual strong group. And it is probably a mistake for a student to try to position himself in the intellect group when it is clear early in his academic career that this group will be difficult to reach. It is probably more strategically viable to aim for one of the other categories.

The second category is a special talent category. This applicant pool include those who have shown dedication, commitment, and high achievement in a given area of activity. This could be in the arts which would include music, painting, photography, and writing. This could also be sports and include all the major athletic areas. Some sports will have more weight than others, because of the general popularity as well as alumni interest. In the Northeast, for example, ice hockey is a very popular sport, and hockey players will do well in select colleges if they have basic academic achievement and high levels of skill in the sports. In the most selective colleges, it is very important to understand that there is a good level of academic ability, as demonstrated by your transcript grades. Your testing scores will be judged with a minimum cutoff for the top schools. Therefore, if you are above this level and show special skills in these sports, your competitiveness is increased. The special talent category is weighted in favor of athletes. If you are a record holder in the 50-meter freestyle in swimming, an all-state quarterback in football, an all-American point guard in basketball, or a strong goalie in soccer or hockey, you have a tremendous leverage in the admissions process. Back in the 1950's—after Harvard lost to Yale by over 50 points in football, President Nathan Pusey told one of the admission committee members to make sure that Harvard recruited some strong football players and to not let the school lose by such a large margin again. MIT and Cal Tech are two highly selective colleges that have no sports recruiting. They admit a class and find out later who can play sports. However, having a special talent in sports and music will be helpful in the overall appraisal of you as a candidate, and gives the admission committee a look at a broader developed human being.

The third category is the family legacy group. This pool of applicants are children of alumni of the various selective colleges. All selective colleges need alumni contributions for the strength of their financial support. As a trade off to the former graduates of the school and in exchange for their support as a group, the admission committee gives their children an edge in the admissions process. This is not a guarantee of admissions to weak students, but it will give the nod to a student who is equally qualified with another student who does not have a parent connection. Some schools will admit legacy cases at twice the level for normal applicants. Some classes will be composed of 15 to 20 percent of children of alumni. These legacy candidates are generally competing against those who are also legacy.

The fourth category is the social conscience group. This group consists of ethnic minorities, especially those that are under-represented at the top schools. In response to the civil rights movement of the 1960s, many colleges changed their admissions requirements so that minority students who were underrepresented in the past had a better chance of being admitted. This was deemed important for the future of society and to create more diversity in the classroom. It was strongly felt that learning is more dynamic and more meaningful when there are diverse views in the class when opinions are expressed. Contemporary scholars have deemed that homogeneous learning with people of the same background as somewhat deficient. Although all applicants are competing with the entire applicant pool, there is greater competition within pools. Therefore, African-Americans, are primarily competing against other African-Americans for entry. The original objective of this goal was to have represented in each class the percentage of a group that roughly equates to that in the general population. This has been achieved by only a few schools, but has come closer at Stanford and University of Virginia. If a school cannot attract enough applicants in a particular ethnic group, the school is inclined to recruit heavily in order to diversify the student body. Hispanics and Native-Americans along with African-Americans are considered under-represented minorities and they are especially recruited. Harvard sends out letters to all African-American students who score high on the PSAT exam. This is a category similar to the legacy group, that you cannot position yourself for but are merely in this group by virtue of birth.

The fifth category is the well-rounded student group. Because the vast majority of the applicant pool fall into this category, it is the most competitive of all the groups. Many students position themselves as being well rounded, thinking this is sufficient to gain entrance into the most selective college. This is not true. Because the competition is so intense in this category, the applicants should try to create a hook or something that catches the attention of the admission committee. Admission officers are bored reading the resumes of well-rounded students. It is important to have an application that wakes up a sleeping admission officer as he reads applications late into the evening. It is common to hear complaints from the admission officers about students who bring average skills to the classroom and make no contribution to the rich discussions of new ideas. Sometimes, additional factors become known to the admission committee through an offhand comment by a teacher recommendation and from other sources. This gives the well-rounded applicant a critical edge in the process. An applicant should work to create and reveal those unusual attributes. It could be something as basic as coming from an area where very few applicants have applied in recent years.

Many admission committees discuss groups of applicants in separate rounds. They also make selections in these rounds with applicants competing with others in the designated category. The best positioning that a student can make in the selective college application process is to enter more than one of the above categories as a competitive candidate. This ensures that the admission committee will discuss you in more than one round. You can meet their needs in two levels, and your application has a better possibility in this super competitive pool. All the categories except the intellects can be considered some form of affirmative action, because they are selected primarily for a reason other than intellectual greatness.

Recommendations and Interviews

"Education is a social process...Education is growth....
Education is, not a preparation for life; education is life itself."

—*John Dewey*

The issue of recommendations is one that any student has to think through very carefully. Most colleges need at least two teachers and one college counselor to write for you. Try to get teachers who have known you for an extended time and teachers whom you have done well with in their courses. You have to make personal contact with the teachers to discuss the recommendation. Be sure to ask them whether they can give you a strong recommendation. Get teachers who are from various types of discipline. Make sure that you have done well in the courses of the teachers you ask. A science and math teacher should complement nicely with an English or history teacher. Make your request to the teacher in writing. Spell out your college objective, by listing the colleges you will apply to and that you have worked closely with the college counselor to develop the list. Also mention that you have visited some of the colleges. Be sure to thank, in writing, teachers when they write recommendations for you.

Be polite all the time and help the teacher by giving envelopes and materials needed for the recommendation. Be sure to ask the teacher early in the admission process so that he can get the work done, before many other students ask as the deadlines approach. Be sure to contact your college after the application has been sent, to make sure it has received all the letters of recommendation and forms that are required. To avoid confusion, make sure that you write your name and the deadline date of the college involved on the envelope before giving it to the teacher.

The application essay

The importance of the college essay should not be underestimated. The essay can make the difference between your gaining acceptance and being rejected. Students have to avoid using a common cliché model of an essay. For example, the essay which explains how you learned about life from your particular sport or repeating things that occur in other parts of the application. An essay could be the marginal difference between acceptance and rejection. Effort and care should be applied to developing and writing your essay. Your writing, whether good or bad, reflects on you as a person or potential student at the college you are applying.

Be careful to avoid a topic that is too broad. It is very difficult to develop a broad topic in 500 words. The committee is looking for the student's unique voice. Make sure that your writing identifies who you are as a unique person.

An essay is an opportunity and a danger. It's an opportunity to project yourself and present a compelling argument for your admission. In recent years, the essay has assumed increasing value as a measure of a student's capabilities. Writing skills are a barometer of an educated citizen. It is ironic that only a small proportion of applicants put as much effort and time in the essay as, for example, the time they spend preparing for the SAT-I.

College admission officers, in the most selective college, state that greater efforts by applicants in preparing their essays can pay off in the positive assessment of the student. Success is linked to your effectiveness in sending a message, the content of the message, and how well the message reveals something special about you.

Demand honesty from yourself. Even if you have to expose a moment of failure, do it honestly and tell what you have learned from the experience that has strengthen and developed you as a person. Focus on issues that are important to you. Explain why the issue is important. Also, focus on one particular area or idea. A big mistake is to attempt to cover many areas and issues in 500 words. It is difficult, and could compromise your chance to maximize the essay portion of your application.

Be careful when bragging and boasting about yourself on an essay. Be modest when making claims about your talents. The facts will speak for themselves and do not require you to embellish them too much. Mention everything, but present it subtly. Be careful with offbeat questions. They can be winners for the clever writer but they can be dangerous for the unprepared writer. Describing a dinner conversation that you would have with five famous people of your choosing is an example of this type of question.

Also be careful if you use humor, and keep it in good taste. Crude humor can offend and signal to the reader a mark of immaturity.

Use good grammar and punctuation. It is advisable to show drafts of your essays to others, including teachers and counselors to get their reaction, opinion, and feedback.

Interview well

Some colleges require interviews but others do not need interviews at all. A candidate should approach an interview in a relaxed state of mine. It's difficult to lose your chances for admission on the basis of an interview. It is highly unlikely that this could happen. An interview confirms what most colleges find in your folder. The main purpose is to obtain additional information about the candidate that is not found in the folder. The interview can provide a platform for the candidate to ask questions about the college. How should you prepare for it? It is quite appropriate to have someone asked you from a list of general questions that may occur during the interview process. Your answers can give you valuable practice in preparing to talk with the interviewer. There may be questions that might overlap but this approach of mock interviews can help you begin to develop talking points that you can elaborate on when the actual interviewer begins the questions.

You should come to the interview very neat and very well dressed. Smile a lot and keep eye contact with the interviewer. Interviews are to be enjoyed as informal conversations where you will let the interviewer get to know you better as a person. An interview is not a test and there's no such thing as a right or wrong answer. If controversial questions are asked, you should give your opinion and be prepared to support it in a logical way.

A candidate should prepare for the interview by going over potential questions and having specific responses in mind that can be given. A good way to practice is to look in the mirror while answering questions. If you can be comfortable doing that, you can definitely deal with looking the interviewer in the eye and answering his questions.

You should also be prepared to ask intelligent questions about the college you are seeking to enter. Do not ask questions that can easily be answered by reading the view book and other college publications. Ask questions that call for personal insight and perspective of the interviewer. If the interviewer is an alumnus of the college, ask him what special meaning that the college has for his career development. Also ask what specific advise he can give you as a potential new student.

In the beginning the interviewer will try to discuss general things to get you relaxed. Later, questions are asked that would give you the opportunity to take the ball and run. Elaborate and give details when responding to questions. Short snappy answers will not suffice. Your job is to tell a story, to tell a compelling story. The objective should be to create in the mind of the interviewer a feeling that you will be a definite asset to the campus you are seeking to join.

Sometimes you'll be interviewed by alumni, admissions office staff, or interviewers who are students at the college in question. All of these different personalities will provide a unique platform for you to express your views and thoughts. Take advantage of this opportunity, if you are asked to answer a question you don't know, be honest and say, "I'd like to think about that," and come back to that question after you have time to mull it over. Candidates will be observed for how they dress or how they present themselves, their level of curiosity, and their intellectual strength and stamina. A good objective in an interview is to get the interviewer to join your team of getting admitted to the school in question. Be a persuasive advocate for yourself and your unique special qualities. The following are sample questions that might come up in an interview, and even if the same questions don't come up getting the answers to these will prepare you for other similar type questions.

Sample questions they may ask you include (practice answering these in front of a mirror):

What would you bring to MIT that's unique and special?

Tell me your strengths and weaknesses?

What are your career plans? What will you major in?

Why are you interested in MIT and what in particular can we offer you?

What would I find is your role in the school community here when you start?

What kind of self-development do you wish to see in yourself in the next four years?

Where and when do you find yourself most stimulated intellectually?

What points about yourself would you like to leave with me so that I can present your strongest side to our committee on admissions?

What events would you deem crucial in your life thus far?

What do you feel sets you apart as an individual in your school?

What have you heard about MIT?

What is your parting comment?

If you were chosen to head your high school what would be your first move?

What would you do with a fresh $20,000 if it were given to you?

I practiced with Mark when he prepared for interviews. As he rode along in the car, I asked questions that might come up in an interview to see how he would respond. He cooperated and gave answers that he might have given in the real interview. Afterwards, I would give him feedback on the answers he gave on how he might improve his performance. This exercise proved very useful because gradually Mark became more confident in having a discussion like this, and he developed more elaborate details as time when on. Most importantly his confidence about being able to interview well increased.

When the admissions process came to a close, he had interviews with about four colleges. His assessment of the success of those interviews was very high. He thought that he established rapport with the interviewer, and that he answered the questions with details while being very comfortable with the process. He made it a point to ask relevant questions about the college to the interviewers and to indicate through his discussion that the college he was being interviewed for was a college he really wanted to attend. He demonstrated this by showing specific knowledge of the college and specific factors about the college which attracted him to it.

Rejections and Wait Lists

"Give a man a fish and you feed him for a day. Teach a man to fish and you feed him for a lifetime."

—*Chinese Proverb*

Rejection is reality

The spring of the senior year is a time of joy and simultaneously a time of depression. Many seniors will walk around in a gloomy mood after they get rejected by their favorite college(sometimes more than one). That's life. Sometimes we do well, and sometimes we will not do well. Psychologically, a student has to prepare for the let down of rejection.

Any rejection letter you receive is not a reflection of your self-worth or your ability to succeed in life. It is primarily a reflection of the strength of the applicant pool you happen to be competing against. Remember, you are competing with some of the best students in the USA and the world. Some students have published papers in math journals, won the national Westinghouse Science Competition, have made music CDs, have set up national organizations, or have published best selling novels.

I stressed, as a parent, the necessity of preparing mentally for the worst-case scenario. By preparing for the worst case, inevitably the let down effect will be lessened. If you succeed, consider it a bonus and enjoy that victory. Take your victories where you find them. However, be prepared for defeat.

For many students, the college-admission season is a very tense and nerve racking time. Parents should consciously try to be supportive and not involve themselves in too much criticism at this time. Reserve criticisms for periods prior to this period and after this period. Parents have to avoid driving students over the edge by adding to the stress with their worries and concerns over admission to the top colleges. The parental role is to show unconditional positive regard and unending support during this time. Parents have to stress their love and make this statement, " no matter what happens and where you get rejected we still love you just the same and respect your achievements as a person and a student."

Wait lists

A wait-list is limbo land for students. It promises nothing but is nice to hear that you are not rejected. It is particularly exasperating to find out that you came very close but did not quite get in. A wait-list response should be seen as an acknowledgement of the student's qualifications but there are limitations in the class size the college can accept. The wait list is set up for the convenience of the college in case it miscalculates the size of the yield, which is the number of students who accept the college. If the yield is lower than expected they can go to the waiting list and pick up a few students to reach the planned class size and keep the right balance among various applicant categories. What should students do as a follow-up? Students should send additional materials to support their application and they should write a letter reaffirming their desire to attend the college. Sit tight on the wait-list, but the probability of a conversion from wait list to acceptance is very low. Be realistic. Choose from the acceptances you get, and move on. Pay the deposit in the best college on your list of acceptances and wait. If you hit the lottery and get the top college to send you a thick envelope, you can contact the college where you have made the deposit and inform them of your decision change. This is not unethical and is an accepted part of the college acceptance game.

Financial Aid

"If a man empties his purse into his head, no man can take it away from him. An investment in knowledge always pays the best interest."

—Benjamin Franklin

The need for financial aid is one of those nearly universal needs for college students. The cost of attending college is at an all time high, and each year the costs increase at a rate greater than the rate of inflation. Without financial aid in the form of grants, loans, and work-study programs, many students would not be able to attend college.

There are two types of financial aid, need-based aid and merit aid. Need-based aid is determined by your family's financial status and prospects. The poorer you are, the more aid you can expect. This is the great equalizer for American society. The idea is to create the upward mobility based on your need. If you have the academic or special skills talent, the most selective colleges will let you in regardless of your socio-economic class. On the other hand, your special skills or your high academic achievement determine merit-based aid. Merit-based aid is difficult to get and is not provided at all by MIT, the Ivy League, and other selected colleges. Many less selective colleges lure excellent students away from the Ivy League by offering grant aid. This has the effect of getting more students off the waiting lists at selective colleges.

Long-term planning is best for optimal success with financial aid. Just as we emphasize long-term planning for success with academic preparation for select colleges, we also stress early and consistent planning for financial success with college. Parents should open, before birth, a special savings fund for college education. The investment vehicle should be geared toward stock funds that are designed for long-term college planning. Be disciplined about putting in a specific amount each month over several years. Investigate with your employer about the possibility of using a 401 (K) plan for college savings. Later, you can borrow from that plan for college costs. The advantage comes through the tax savings and the ruling that 401 (K) amounts are not used to determine how much parents have to contribute to college costs.

Students should learn early about the costs of education and the sacrifices that the family must make to pay those costs. As students learn the value of a college education, they develop a respect for it and may focus their energies more on performing well academically. Students are strongly encouraged to save their money and put it away for their college education. It should be saved in the parent's name to keep control over the use of the money at the parental level through college. This avoids the purchase of the red Ferrari syndrome, or a wayward student turning the money over to a cult. Students are also encouraged to research the process of getting external scholarships. These can be a great source of money and might involve many applications and the mailing of many letters in the search effort. Some scholarships, such as the Coca Cola Scholarship, are very competitive and several hundred thousand students compete for a handful of awards.

In order to qualify for financial aid, students have to 1) be a US citizen or permanent resident; 2) demonstrate eligibility for receiving specific types of aid; 3) have a high school diploma or its equivalent; 4) enroll in a school participating in the Federal Student Aid Program; 5) possess a social security number; 6) show satisfactory academic progress in their school grades; 7) sign a statement of educational purpose and a certification statement on overpayment and default; and 8) register with the Selective Service if required.

Aid is awarded on the basis of need. The information you supply is used in a formula to calculate your Expected Family Contribution (EFC). The formula is as follows.

Cost of attendance - Expected Family Contribution (EFC)= Financial Need

In general, Federal Financial Aid is limited to certain dollar amounts at participating colleges. Submitting applications on time is critical to optimizing the chances of getting this aid. Grants and scholarships are the best form of aid because they do not have to be paid back. Whereas, Federal Student Loans can provide funds to all eligible students, but they have to be paid back. The types of financial aid are as follows:

Federal Pell Grants are available to students if the family-expected contribution is less that $2,100.The grant amount depends on the *Expected Family Contribution.*

Federal Supplemental Educational Opportunity Grant (FSEOG) is for students of exceptional financial need and priority is given to Federal Pell Grant recipients. The total amount received can reach $4000 for those with maximum need.

Federal Work Study (FWS) facilitates undergraduate students getting jobs during their academic year of study. These jobs typically have a limited amount of hours and can be either on or off campus. These jobs on some campuses can result in valuable contacts and add useful references to the resume. MIT students can do research with Nobel Prize winners.

Federal Perkins Loans are loans with low interest and are usually paid back after the student finishes school. The maximum amount one can borrow is about $3000 and repayment must begin nine months after the student graduates.

Federal Stafford Loans are another loan program with a slightly higher interest rate than the Perkins Loan. The maximum amount one can borrow changes from year to year and the loan is also available to students who study at least half time.

Federal Plus Loans are available to the parents rather than the student, who want to borrow federal funds for the education of their children. Good credit is essential and repayment begins 60 days after disbursement.

Private financial aid is available from a variety of sources including banks, credit unions and student loan organizations. A popular private source of money is the EXCEL program from Nellie Mae. Contact them at 1-800-634-9308.

Another private source of loans is the Achiever Loan. Borrowers must demonstrate credit-worthiness and the ability to pay. Loan amounts can range from $2000 to the total cost of education. Interest rates can vary quarterly. Repayment begins 30 days after loan disbursement and can take up to 20 years for repayment. Contact Key Education resources at 1-800-KEY-LEND.

The application for all the Federal programs is called the Free Application for Federal Student Aid (FAFSA). This must be completed by the student and the parents. The admission counselors in your school can provide you with these forms. All deadlines associated with this form should be adhered to and met in order to insure that money will be available for you.

You also need to fill out a form called the College Scholarship Service Profile Form (CSSP). This is an organization that produces a customized application packet after you send in the registration form. This customized application has to be filled out by the candidate and mailed out before the deadline designated by the school you are applying to. This form is required by most colleges and helps to determine your financial need.

Summary of Admissions

"Without education, you're not going anywhere in this world."

—Malcolm X

Getting into a selective college

Begin preparing yourself in elementary, junior high, and high school. It is not too early to begin to develop the habits that will make you a strong contender when you apply. Develop the habit of getting A's in your courses. Learn what it takes to get the top grade. High grades can be earned by those who are smart and also earned by those who work diligently. When you establish the track record of getting A's, the teacher will grow to expect that from you and the subsequent A's will be easier to make.

Take the toughest courses that are offered in your school. Although you may make B's in some of these courses, these grades will be more respected than an A from a mediocre course. To a large extent, the colleges will evaluate your high school in determining whether the courses are rigorous by their standards. If you are attending one of the magnet high schools in your state, then any courses in that school will gain respect from the admission offices.

Make sure that your SAT results are as high as you can make them. Colleges will say that this is only a number and that they pay more attention to the grades, however, there are clear messages sent by either a high SAT or a low SAT score. That message is clear, if you are below the cut-offs for admission they can deliver you a rejection letter a few months later. It does not hurt, and it can possibly be crucial to your success to take the SAT preparatory course. The best strategy is to start early in junior high, taking the SAT for practice and develop the long-term perspective and skills utilizing the techniques of various offers to master this test. It is a very important test and should not be taken lightly.

In your applications, show how you will bring special characteristics to the school. Make sure you point out any unique aspects of your background, parent, and family history. If you have done something unique, do not hide this from the admission committee. Tell the school what you will bring to the table. If you have traveled in some unusual places, worked at a special job, organized and began some community service project, or developed a special unique skill, make sure that the admission committee knows.

When you select your extracurricular activities, make sure that you are actively involved and that you became an officer of that particular organization. Mere membership or casual involvement with several organizations will not be accepted as a true case of committed activity.

Make sure that the teachers who recommend you have agreed to give you a robust recommendation, which is compelling to the admission committee. If you have been involved in special projects like scouting, get an additional letter from your scoutmaster who can explain more dimensions of you to the committee. If a teacher cannot give you a strong recommendation, politely tell him that you need to find someone who can, then go to another teacher.

Make a big effort to do well on your interviews. Interviews may not be a single factor which can get you an invitation, but it is one of many factors that can keep you out of a top college. Therefore, don't underestimate the importance of the interview. Prepare for it carefully and practice for it. Make a list of questions that you can answer that would be typical of interviews. Dress well and neatly, and arrive to the interview on time. Try to be very relaxed, and provide ample details to the interviewer so that you will not be judged on limited information. Avoid asking questions in an interview which are answered in the school brochures.

Show the school why it's the best place for you. Clearly communicate that the school is your first choice, and that both the institution and you will benefit from your presence on campus. Point out your activity on a contemporary issue and how you will bring this energy and enthusiasm to the next campus.

Send applications out early in the mail. If you are applying for early action or early decision, that can be a decided advantage in the application process. Find the one school that you are very interested in and get an early decision or early action application off as quickly as possible. Get your applications off before the crowd arrives; they'll be more fresh and able to give you the time and concentration that your detail presentation deserves.

Honesty in the information you provide to school, via the application and interview, is imperative. The information should be truthful and honest. You do not need to provide documentation for everything you did, the mere statement of that in your application will be trusted by the admission officer.

Making decisions

Once the letters arrive from the colleges, hopefully you will have good colleges to choose to attend in the fall. The process has not ended yet. A student has to make careful decisions about which college to attend. Financial aid packages have to be evaluated and another visit to the colleges may be necessary. Once the decision is made after thorough research and discussion with family, a letter along with your deposit stating that you plan to attend in the fall is now required. Letters should also be sent to all the other colleges that accept you letting them know that you will not attend. This will permit students on the waiting list to be notified.

If all goes well you will be happy in the spring of your senior year of high school and well prepared to matriculate at MIT or any other selective college in America. More importantly, you will be prepared for life.

About the Author

The author presently resides with his wife in Portland, Oregon. He previously was Associate Professor at King Saud University and formerly a member and chairperson of the Board of Trustees at the American International School in Riyadh, Saudi Arabia. He was educated at Morehouse College, Bowdoin College, University of Pennsylvania, University of California at Berkeley and Harvard University. He specialized in Epidemiology, Dental Medicine and Public Health. The author has two sons who graduated from the International School in Riyadh. Mark graduated from Phillips Academy in Andover, Massachusetts, and is now attending the Massachusetts Institute of Technology in Cambridge, Massachusetts; Geoffrey graduated from Choate Rosemary Hall in Wallingford, Connecticut, and is now attending Williams College in Williamstown, Massachusetts.

http://members.home.net/eguile/secrets/

Parenting Bibliography

Albert, Linda. *Coping with Kids and School (1984)*, E.P. Dutton.

Amabile, Teresa. *Growing Up Creative, Nurturing a Lifetime of Creativity (1992)*, Creative Education Foundation.

American Academy of Pediatrics. Pediatric Nutrition Handbook (1993).

Ames, Louise Bates. *He Hit Me First (1989)*, Warner Banks.

Anderson, Joan. *Teen is a Four-Letter Word, A Survival Kit for Parents (1983)*, Better Way.

Armstrong, Thomas. *In Their Own Way. Discovering and Encouraging Your Childs Personal Learning Style (1987)*, Tarter.

Arp, Claudia. *Beating the Winter Blues: The Complete Survival Handbook for Moms (1991)*, Nelsen.

Arterburn, Stephen. *Drug-Proof Your Kids (1989)*, Focus on the Family.

Baker, S. and Henry, *R.R. Parents' Guide to Nutrition (1986)*, Addison-Wesley

Barnes, Robert Jr. *Who's in Charge Here? Overcoming Power Struggles with Your Kids (1990).*

Bennett, Steve and Ruth. *365 TV-Free Activities You Can Do with Your Child (1991)*, Bob Adams, Inc.

Benson, Peter. *The Quicksilver Years: Hopes and Fears of Early Adolescence (1987)*, Harper & Row.

Bergstrom, Joan. *School's Out-Now What? Creative Choices for Your Child (1984)*, Ten Speed Press.

Bettelheim, Bruno. *A Good Enough Parent (1987)*, Vintage Books.

Bloom, Alan. *The Closing of the American Mind (1988)*, Simon & Schuster.

Brazelton, T. Berry. *On Becoming a Family (1981)*, Delacoto Press.

Brazelton, T. Berry. *Toddlers and Parents (1986)*, Dell Publishers.

Brazelton, T. Berry. *Working and Caring (1985)*, Addison-Wesley.

Brown, Jean. *Keeping Your Kids Safe (1985)*, Monarch Press.

Bustanoby, David. *Tough Parenting for Dangerous Times (1992),* Zondervan.

Calano, Jimmy and Salzman, Jeff. *Careertracking* (1988) Simon and Schuster

Calderone, Mary S., M.D. and Johnson, Eric W. *The Family Book About Sexuality.*

Calkins, McCormick. *The Art of Teaching Writing (1986),* Heinemann.

Canter, Lee. *Assertive Discipline for Parents (1988),* Harper & Row.

Canter, Lee. *Homework without Tears (1988),* Harper & Row.

Carlson, Richard. *Celebrate Your Child: The Art of Happy Parenting (1992),* New World Library.

Clabby and Elias. *Teach Your Child Decision Making (1987),* Doubleday.

Cohen, Marion. *Marijuana: Its Effects on Mind and Body (1985),* Chelsea House.

Corkille-Briggs, Dorothy. *Your Childs Self-Esteem,* Doubleday & Co.

Crary, Elizabeth. Pick *Up Your Socks and Other Skills Growing Children Need! (1990),* Parenting Press, Inc.

Craven, Linda. *Stepfamilies. New Patterns of Harmony (1982),* Messner.

Davidson, Christine. *Staying Home Instead: How to Quit the Working Mom Rat Race and Survive Financially (1986),* Lexington Books.

Davitz, Lois Jean. *How to Live (Almost) Happily with a Teenager (1982),* Winston Press.

DeSisto, A. Michael. *Decoding Your Teenager. How to Understand Each Other During the Turbulent Years* (1991), William Marrow & Co.

DiGuilm, Robert. *Effective Parentin*g (1980), Follett Publishing.

Dinkmeyer, Don. *Raising a Responsible* Child (1982), Simon & Schuster.

Dobson, James. *The Strong-Willed Child: Birth Through Adolescence (1984)*, Tyndale House Publishers.

Dobson, James. *Parenting Isn't for Cowards* (1987), Word Publishing.

Dodson, Fitzhugh. *How to Single Parent* (1987), Harper & Row.

Elkind, David. *The Hurried Child* (1988), Addison-Wesley.

Elkind, David. *Miseducation: P*reschoolers at *Risk* (1987), Knopf.

Eyre, Linda. *Teaching Children Responsibility* (1982), Ballantine Books.

Faber, *Adele. Siblings Without Rivalry* (1987), Avon Books.

Faber, Adele. *How to Talk So Kids Will Listen and Listen So Kids Will Talk* (1980), Avon Books.

Feiden, Karyn. *Parents' Guide to Raising Responsible Kids: Preschool Through Teen Years* (1990), Prentice-Hall.

Ferber, Richard. *Solve* Your *Child's Sleep Problems* (1986), Simon & Schuster.

Fraiberg, Selmm. *The Magic Years* (1959-a classic), Charles Scribner's Sons.

Fuller, Cheri. *Motivating Your Kids from Crayons to Career* (1990), Honor Books.

Galbraith, Judy. *The Gifted Kids Survival Guide (1987)*, Free Spirit Publishing.

Gale, Jay. *A* Young *Woman's Guide to Sex* (1988), Body Press.

Gale, Jay. *A Young Man's Guide to* Sex (1988), Body Press.

Galinsky, Ellen. *The Six Stages of Parenthood (1987)*.

Gerson, K. *Hard Choices: How Women Decide About Career and Motherhood (1985)*, University of California Press.

Gong and Rudnick. *AIDS: Facts and* Issues (1987), Rutgers University Press.

Gordon, Sol. *Raising a Child Conservatively in a Sexually Permissive* World (1986), Simon & Schuster.

Gorman and Diu. *Breaking the Cycle of Addiction: A Parents Guide to Raising Healthy Kids* (1987) Health Communications.

Goleman, Daniel. *Emotional Intelligence* (1995), Bantam.

Greene and Minton. *Twelve Winning Ways to College Admission* (1987), Little & Brown.

Gregg, Elizabeth and Judith Knotts. *Growing Wisdom, Growing Wonder (1980)*, MacMillan.

Greydamis, Donald E., M.D. *Caring for Your Adolescent- Ages* 12 *to* 21 (1991), Bantam Books.

Grief, Geoffrey. *Single Fathers* (1985), Lexington Books.

Grossman, Linda M., PhD and Deborah Kowal, M.A. *Kids, Drugs, and Sex: Preventing Trouble.*

Guarendi, Raymond. *Back to the Family: Proven Advice on Building* a *Stronger, Healthier, Happier Family* (1991), Simon & Schuster.

Hale-Bensen, Janice E. *Black Children: Their Roots, Culture, and Style* (1986), Johns Hopkins.

Hart, Louise. *The Winning Family: Increasing Self-Esteem in Your Children and Yourself (1987)*, Dodd, Mead.

Hearne, Betsy. *Choosing Books for Children.*

Hechinger, Grace. *How to Raise a Street-Smart Child. The Complete Parents' Guide to Safety on the Street and at Home (1985)*, Fawcett.

Heins and Seden. *Child Can, Parent Can (1987)*, Doubleday.

Herskowitz, Joel. *Is Your Child Depressed? (1988)*, Pharos Books.

Hirsch, Rowena. *Super Working Mom's Handbook (1986)*, Warner Books.

Howard, Marion. *How to Help Your Teen Postpone Sexual Involvement (1987)*, National Academy.

Huchton, Laura. *Protect Your Child (1985)*, Prentice-Hall.

Huggins, Kevin. *Parenting Adolescents (1989)*, NavPress.

Issues and Stoll. *Who's in Control? A Parent's Guide to Discipline (1986)*, Putnam.

Kersey, Katharine C. *The Art of Sensitive Parenting (1983)*, Acropolis.

Kersey, Katherine C. *Helping Your Child Handle Stress (1985)*, Acropolis.

Ketterman, Grace, M.D. *How to Teach Your Children About Sex.*

Klagsbrun, Francine. Too *Young to Die (1984)*, Simon & Schuster.

Kranyik, Margery. *How to Help Your 3 to 8-Year-Old Make the Most of School (1982)*, Continuum.

Kuntzleman, Charles. *Healthy Kids for Life (1988)*, Simon & Schuster.

Kurshan, Neil. *Raising Your Child to Be a Decent Responsible Person (1987)*, Atheneum.

LaFountain, William, *Setting Limits: Parents, Kids, & Drugs (1982)*, Hamilton.

Lansky, Vicki. *Practical Parenting Tips: Over 1500 Helpful Hints for the First Five Years (1980)*, Meadowbrook Press.

Lansky, Vicki. *101 Ways to Tell Your Child "I Love You" (1988)*, Contemporary Books.

Lappe, Frances. *After You Turn Off the TV Set: Fresh Ideas for Family Time (1985)*, Ballantine Press.

Laskin, David. *Parents Book for New Fathers (1988)*, Ballantine Books.

Leach, Penelope. *Your Baby and Child (1977)*, Knopf.

Leach, Penelope. *Your Growing Child (1983)*, Knopf.

Leman, Dr. Kevin. *Making Children Mind Without Losing* Yours *(1984)*, Revell.

Leman, Dr. Kevin. Sex *Begins in the Kitchen.*

LeShan, Eda. *When Your Child Drives You* Crazy *(1985)*, St. Martin's Press.

Marone, Nicky. *How to Father a Successful Daughter (1987)*, McGraw-Hill.

Martin, D. *Good Times with Health and Safety (1983)*, Colorado State University: Cooperative Extension Service.

Mayo, Mary Ann. *Parent's Guide to Sex Education.*

McCoy and Wibbelsman. *Growing and Changing. A Handbook for Preteens (1986)*, Perigree Books.

Minear, Ralph E. *Kids' Symptom: From Birth to Teen* (1992), Avon Books.

Nelson, Christine A. *Should I Call the Doctor?* (1986), Warner Books.

Newman, Susan. *You Can Say No to a Drink or Drug* (1986), Putnam.

Oppenheim, Joarme. *Raising a Confident Child* (1985), Pantheon Books.

Osman, Betty. *Learning Disabilities: A Family Affair* (1979), Random House.

Pappas, Michael. *Sweet Dreams* for *Little Ones, Bedtime Fantasies to Build Self-Esteem,* Winston Press.

Peck, Scott. *The Road Less Traveled* (1985), Simon & Schuster.

Pool, Kathy. A *Mothers Manual for Summer Survival* (1989), Focus on the Family.

Penner, Clifford & Joyce. *Sex Facts for the Family* (1986), Word Publishing.

Perino and Perino. *Parenting the Gifted & Developing the Promise* (1981), Bowker Company.

Quinn, P.E. *The Golden Rule of Parenting: Using Discipline Wisely* (1986), Abingdon Press.

Reit, Seymour V. *Sibling Rivalry* (1985), Ballantine Books.

Reuben, Steven Care. *But How Will You Raise the Children? A Guide to Interfaith Marriage* (1987),Pocket Books.

Ricci, L. *Mom's House, Dad's House* (1982), MacMillan.

Rimrn, Sylvia. *Underachievement Syndrome: Causes and Cures* (1986), Apple Publishing.

Rodgers and Cataldo. *Raising Sons: Practical Strategies for Single Mothers (1984)*, New American Library.

Roles, Eric. *The Kid's Book about Death and Dying* (1985), Little Brown.

Rogers and Head. *Mister Rogers' How Families Grow* (1988), Berkley Books.

Rosemond, John. *Ending the Homework Hassle* (1990), Andrews & McMeel.

Rosamond, John. *Six-Point Plan for Raising Happy, Healthy Children* (1989).

Rosemond, John. *Parent Power!* (1990), Andrews & McMeel.

Salter, E. *How to Get Your Kid to Eat But Not Too Much (1987)*, Bull Publishing Co.

Samalin, N. and Morthan, J. *Loving Your Child is Not Enough* (1987), Viking Penguin, Inc.

Sanford, Linda. *The Silent Children: The Parent's Guide to the Prevention of Child Sexual Abuse* (1982), McGraw-Hill.

Sanger and Kelly. *The Woman Who Works, The Parent Who Cares* (1987), Little, Brown, & Co.

Schaefer, Charles E. *Raising Baby Right (1991).*

Schuller, Robert Harold. *Power Ideas for a Happy Family (1972)*, Fleming H. Revell Co.

Schwartzman, Michael. *The Anxious Parent.*

Sam, William. *Nighttime Parenting (1990)*, La Leche League International.

Seldman, Martin L. *Performance without Pressure* (1988), Walker.

Shallcross, Doris. *Teaching Creative Behavior (1985)*, Bearly Ltd.

Shelov, Steven P., M.D. *Caring for Your Baby and* Young *Child (1991)*, Bantam Books.

Shiff, E. *Experts Advise Parents: A Guide to Raising Loving, Responsible Children (1987)*, Delacorte Press.

Shore, Kermeth. The *Special Education Handbook (1986)*, Harper & Row.

Siegel, Brisman, and Weinshel. *Surviving an Eating Disorder.- New Perspectives and Strategies for Family and Friends (1988)*, Harper & Row.

Silberstein, Muriel. *Doing Art Together (1983)*, Simon & Schuster.

Singer, Dorothy, *Getting the Most Out of TV (1981)*, Scott Foresman.

Steinberg, Lawrence. *Adolescent Development (1984)*, Alfred Knopf,

Stevens, Suzanne. *The Learning Disabled Child: Ways That Parents Can Help.*

Stoppard, Miriam. *Baby and Child A to Z Medical Handbook.*

Sullivan, Maria. *The Parent/Child Manual on Divorce (1988)*, St. Martin's Press.

Swibart, Judson. *How to Treat Your Family as Well as You Treat Your Friends (1982)*, Regal Books.

Taylor, John F. The *Hyperactive Child and the Family—The Complete What-to-Do Handbook* (1987),Dodd Publishers,

Trelease, Jim. *The Read-Aloud Handbook (1982)*, Penguin.

Urban, Hal. 20 *Things I Want My Kids to Know: Passing On Life's Greatest Lessons (1992)*, Nelson.

Visher and Visher. *How to Win as a Stepfamily (1982)*, Dembner.

White, Burton L. *The First Three* Years *of Life (1975)*, Prentice-Hall.

Wiener, Harvey S. *Any Child Can Read Better.*

Wilson, Sandra D. *Shame-Free Parenting (1992)*, Inter Varsity Press.

Winn, Marie. *Unplugging the Plug-in Drug (1987)*, Viking.

Winn, Marie. *Children Without Childhood (1983)*, Pantheon.

Winston-Hiller, Randy. *Some Secrets are for Sharing (1986)*, MacMillan.

Waititz, Janet G. *Healthy Parenting: An Empowering Guide for Adult Children* (1992*)*, Simon & Schuster.

Wolfson, Randy-M. and Virginia DeLuca. *Couples with Children (1981)*, Dembner Books.

Wood, Barry. *Questions Teenagers Ask about Dating and* Sex.

Wyckoff, Jerry and Barbara C. Unell. Discipline Without Shouting or Spanking (1984), Meadowbrook.

Ziglar, Zig. *Raising Positive Kids in a Negative World (1985),* Nelson.

General Learning References and Reading List

Adler, Mortimer J. *A Guidebook to Learning: For the Lifelong Pursuit of Wisdom*, New York: Macmillan Publishing Co.,1986.

Adler, Mortimer J. *Six Great Ideas. New* York: Macmillan Publishing Co., 1981.

Adler, Mortimer J. *The Paideia Proposal.* New York: Macmillan Publishing Co., 1982.

Anderson, Barry F. *The Complete Thinker: A Handbook of Techniques for Creative and Critical Problem Solving.* Englewood Cliffs, New Jersey: Prentice-Hall, 1980.

Arnold, John. *The Art of Decision-Making.* New York: AMACOM, 1978.

Bandler, Richard, and Grinder, John. *Frogs into Princes,* Moab, UT: Real People Press, 1979.

Barnhart, Robert K., ed. *The Barnhart Dictionary of Etymology.* W. Wilson, *1988.*

Barrett, Susan L. *It's All in Your Head: A Guide to Understanding Your Brain and Boosting Your Brain Power.* -.Minneapolis, Minnesota: Free Spirit Publishing Co., 1985.

Bates, Jefferson. *Dictating Effectively.* Washington, DC Acropolis Books, 1986.

Benham, Sir William Gurney. *Benham's Book of Quotations, Proverbs and Household Words.* New York: Putnam's, 1949.

Blanchard, Kenneth, and Spencer Johnson. *The One Minute Manager.* New York: William Morrow and Co. Inc., 1981.

Blanchard, Kenneth, Patricia Zigarmi and Drea Zigarmi. *Leadership and the One Minute Manager.* New York: William Morrow and Co. Inc., 1985.

Bliss, Edwin C. *Doing It Now.* New York: Charles Scribner's Sons, 1983.

Bloom, Allan. *The Closing of the American Mind: How Higher Education Has Failed Democracy and Impoverished the Souls Of Today's Students.* NewYork: Simon and Schuster, 1987.

Bloom, Benjamin *S. Developing Talent in Young People.* New York: Ballantine Books, 1985.

Bramson, Robert. *Coping with Difficult People.* Garden City, NY: Anchor Press, 1981.

Brussell, Eugene E. *Dictionary of Quotable Definitions.* Englewood Cliffs, N.J.: Prentice-Hall, 1970.

Burka, Jane and Lenora Yuen. *Procrastination.* Reading, MA: Addison-Wesley, 1985.

Burley-Allen, Madelyn. *Listening, the Forgotten Skill.* New York: John Wiley and Sons, 1982.

Burns, David D. *Feeling Good: The New Mood Therapy.* NewYork: William Morrow and Co., 1980.

Buzen, Tony. *Make the Most of Your Mind.* New York: Simon and Schuster, 1984.

Buzen, Tony. *Use Both Sides of Your* Brain. New York: E.P. Dutton, 1976.

Calvin, William H., and George A. Ojemann. *Inside the Brain.* Bergenfield, New Jersey: The New American Library, 1980.

Carlzon, Jan. *Moments of Truth.* Cambridge, MA: Ballinger Publishing Co., 1987.

Ciardi, John. *Good Words to You.* New York:Harper Row, *1987.*

Claiborne, Robert. *The Roots of English.* New York: Harper Row, 1987.

Clance, Pauline Rose. *The Imposter Phenomenon: When Success Makes You Feel Like a Fake.* New York: Bantam Books, 1986.

Clendening, Corinne P. and Ruth Ann Davies. *Creating Programs for the Gifted; Guide for Teachers, Librarians, and Students..* New York: R.R. Bowker Co., 1980.

Cohen, Herb. You *Can Negotiate Anything.* Don Mills, ON: Lyle Stuart Inc., 1980.

Coleman, Laurence J. *Schooling the Gifted.* New York: Addison Wesley Publishing 1985.

Coles, Robert. *The Moral Life of Children.* Boston: The Atlantic Monthly Press, 1986.

Collinge, N.E. *An Encyclopedia of Language.*2 vols. New York: Routledge, 1989.

Combs, Arthur W. *Myths in Education: Beliefs that Hinder Progress and Their Alternatives.* Boston: Allyn and Bacon, Inc., 1979.

Coplin, William D. and Michael K. O'Leary. *Power Persuasion.* Reading, MA: Addison-Wesley, 1985.

Counts, George S. *Dare the Schools Build a New Social Order?* New York: John Day Co., 1932.

Cox, June, Neil Daniel, and Bruce 0. Boston. *Educating Able Learners: Programs and Promising Practices.* Austin, Texas: University of Texas Press, 1985.

Cutler, Wade E. *Triple Your Reading Speed.* New York: Arco Publishing Inc., 1970.

de Bono, Edward. *Lateral Thinking: A Textbook of Creativity.* New York: Penguin Books, 1977.

de Bono, Edward. *The Five Day Course in Thinking.* New York: Basic Books, 1967.

de Bono, Edward. *The Happiness Purpose.* New York: Penguin Books, 1979.

Delisle, James and Judy Galbraith. *The Gifted Kids Survival Guide.* Minneapolis: Free Spirit Publishing, 1987.

DeVinne, Pamela, ed. *American Heritage Illustrated Encyclopedic Dictionary.* Boston, Mass.: Houghton Mifflin, 1982.

Doyle, Michael and David Strauss. *How to Make Meetings* Work. New York: The Berkley Publishing Group, 1976.

Dyer, Wayne. *Your Erroneous Zones.* New York: Avon Books, 1976.

Erickson, Steve M. *Management Tools for Everyone.* New York: Petrocelli Books, 1981.

Fifield, William. *In Search of Genius.* New York: William Morrow and Co., Inc., 1982.

Flexner, Stuart Berg, ed. *The Random House Dictionary of the English Language.* New York: Random House, 1987.

Galbraith, Ronald E. and Thomas M. Jones. Moral *Reasoning: A Teaching Handbook for Adapting Kohlberg to the Classroom.*New York: Greenhaven Press, 1976.

Gawain, Shakti. *Creative Visualization.* New York: Bantam Books,1978.

Geneen, Harold, with Alvin Moscow. *Managing.* Garden City, NY: Doubleday & Co. Inc., 1984.

Gilligan, Carol. *In a Different Voice: Psychological Theory and Women's Development.* Cambridge, Massachusetts: Harvard University Press, 1982.

Goertzel, V. and M. Goertzel. *Cradles of Eminence.* Boston: Little, Brown, and Co., 1978.

Gordon, William J. J. *Synectics: The Development of Creative Capacity.* New York: Collier Books, 1968.

Gove, Phillip B., ed. *Webster's Third New International Dictionary Unabridged.* New York: G. & C Merriam, 1976.

Gowen, John Curtis, Joe Nhatena, and E. Paul Torrance. *Educating the Ablest.* Itasca, IL: F.E. Peacock Publishers, Inc.,1979.

Grost, A. *Genius in Residence.* Englewood Cliffs, New Jersey, Prentice-Hall, 1971.

Grun, Bernard. *The Timetables of History,* New York: Simon and Schuster, 1979.

Harrison, Allen and Robert M. Branson. *Styles of Thinking: Strategies for Asking Questions, Making Decisions, and Solving Problems.* Garden City, New York: Anchor Press/Doubleday, 1982.

Harvey, Joan C. *If I'm So Successful, Why Do I Feel Like A Fake? The Imposter Phenomenon.*

NewYork, New York: Pocket Books, a division of Simon & Schuster, Inc., 1986.

Hill, Napoleon. *Think and Grow Rich.* New York: Fawcett Crest, 1983.

Hirsch, E.D. Jr. *Cultural Literacy: What Every American Needs to Know.* Boston: Houghton Mifflin, 1987.

Hutchison, Michael. *Megabrain.* New York: Random House, 1986.

Keirsey, David and Marilyn Bates. *Please Understand Me: Character and Temperament Types.* Del Mar, CA: Prometheus Nemesis,1984.

King, Anita, comp. and ed. *Quotations in Black.* Westport, Conn: Greenwood Press, 1981.

Kirst, Werner and Ulrich Diekmeyer. *Creativity Training: Become Creative in 30 Minutes a Day.* New York: Peter H. Wyden Inc., 1973.

Kohlberg, Lawrence. *The Philosophy of Moral Development, Vol. 1.* San Francisco: Harper & Row, 1981.

Lakein, Alan. How *to Get Control of Your Time and Your Life.* New York: The New American Library, 1973.

LeMay, H. Lerner, S. and Taylor M. *New Words.* New York: Facts on File, 1988.

Lickona, Thomas. *Raising Good Children: Helping Your Child Through the Stages of Moral Development from Birth Through - the Teenage Years.* New York: Bantam Books, 1983.

Lipman, Matthew, and Ann Margaret Sharp. *Growing Up With Philosophy.* Philadelphia: Temple University Press, 1978.

Mackenzie, R. Alec. *The Time Trap.* New York: McGraw Hill, 1972.

Magill, Frank N., ed. *Magill's Quotations in Context.* 2 vols. New York: Salem Press, 1965.

Mattox, B. *Getting it Together: Dilemmas for the Classroom* San Diego: Pennant Press, 1975.

Milgram, Stanley. *Obedience to Authority.* New York: Harper & Row 1974.

Montessori, Maria. *The Absorbent Mind.* New York: Dell Publishing Co., Inc., 1984.

Morley, C., ed. *Familiar Quotations by John Bartlett.* Boston, Mass.: Little, Brown, 1948.

Morris, M., and Morris, W. *Dictionary of Word and Phrase Origins.* 2 vols. New York: Harper & Row.

Murray, A.H. et.al ., eds. *The Oxford English Dictionary.* 13 vols. Oxford: Clarendon Press, 1961.

Murray, Sir James Augustus Henry. *New English Dictionary of Historical Principles.* 10 vols. And supplement, Oxford: Clarendon Press, *1888-1933.*

Neustadt, Richard E. and Ernest R. May. *Thinking in Time: The Uses of History for Decision Makers.* New York: The Free Press.

Onions, C.T., ed. *The Oxford Dictionary of English Etymology.* Oxford: Clarendon Press, *1966.*

Oxford Dictionary of Quotations. New York: Oxford University Press, 1986.

Partnow, Elaine, comp. and ed. *The Quotable Woman, 1800-1981.* New York: Facts on File, 1982. (Division of Macmillan), 1986.

Rimm, Sylvia B. *Underachievement Syndrome: Causes and Cures.* Watertown, WI: Apple Publishing Company, 1986.

Roberts, Kate Louise, ed. *Hoyt's New Cyclopedia of Practical Quotations.* New York: Funk and Wagnals, 1964.

Salupo, Victor. *The BS Syndrome: How to Uncover it. Fight it. Master it.* Cleveland: The Bull Buster Press, 1985.

Shipley, Joseph T. *The Origin of English Words* Baltimore, Md.: Johns Hopkins University Press, *1984.*

Stanford, G. and B. Stanford. *Learning Discussion Skills Through Games.* New York: Citation Press, *1969.*

Taylor T. Roger. *Advanced Curriculum Design for Gifted and High Achieving Students Resource Handbook,* Paso Robles, CA: Bureau of Education and Research, 1982.

Taylor, T. Roger. *Building a Quality Program for Gifted Students Resource Handbook*, Paso Robles, CA: Bureau of Education and Research, 1982.

College Admission References

100 Successful College Application Essays, Christopher J. Georges and Gigi E. Georges, Plume Books, New York, NY.

50 College Admission Directors Speak to Parents, Sandra F. MacGowan and Sarah M. McGinty, Harcourt, Brace, Jovanovich PNY Publishers, New York, NY.

ACT: American College Testing Program, Joan U. Levy and Norman Levy, Arco Publishing, New York, NY.

AFI Guide to College Courses in Film and Television, American Film Institute, Arco Publishing, New York, NY.

Applying to Colleges and Universities in the United States: A Handbook for International Students Andrea E. Lehman, Peterson's Guides, Princeton, NJ.

Barron's Index of College Majors, Barron's Educational Series, Happauge, NY.

Barron's Profiles of American Colleges, Barron's Educational Series, Happauge, NY.

Behind the Scenes: An Inside Look at the Selective College Admission Process, Edward B. Wall, Octameron Associates, Alexandria, Va.

Callahan's Guide to Athletics and Academics in America, Timothy R. Callahan, Harper and Row Publishers, New York, NY.

Campus Bound! Annette Spence, Price Stern Sloan, Los Angeles, CA.

Campus Opportunities for Students with Learning Differences, Judith M. Crooker, Octameron Associates, Alexandria, VA.

Campus Pursuit: How to Make the Most of the College Visit and Interview, G. Gary Ripple, Octameron Associates, Alexandria, VA.

Campus Visits and College Interviews: A Complete Guide for College-Bound Students and Their Families, Zola Dincin Schneider, College Board, New York, NY.

Choosing a College: A Guide for Parents and Students, Thomas Sowell, Harper and Row Publishers ,New York, NY.

Choosing a College: The Student's Step-by-Step Decision Making Workbook, Gordon Porter Miller, College Board, New York, NY.

Cliffs Enhanced ACT Preparation Guide, Jerry Bobrow, Cliffs Notes, Lincoln, NY.

Comparative Guide To American Colleges, Jerry Cass and Max Birnbattin, Harper and Publishers, New York, NY.

College Admissions Data Handbook, Orchard IL. College Board, New York, NY.

College Admissions Face to Face, Ann S. Utterback, Seven Locks Press, Cabin John, MD.

College Admissions Index of Majors and Sports, Orchard House, Concord, MA.

College Admissions: A Handbook for Students and Parents, Joan V. Levy and Norman Levy, Arco Publishing, New York, NY.

Consider a Christian College, Christian College Coalition, Peterson's Guides, Princeton, NJ.

Countdown to College: Every Student's Guide to Getting the Most Out of High School, Zola Dincin Schneider and Phyllis B. Kalb, College Board, New York, NY.

Dance Magazine College Guide, Dance Magazine, Inc., New York, NY.

Destination: College, Barbara G, Heyman, Warner Books, New York, NY.

Director of Theater Training, Jill Charles, American Theater Works, Dorset, VT.

Directory of Art and Music Colleges. Roberta Carr, The College Connection, Flushing, New York

Do It Write: How to Prepare a Great College Application G. Gary Ripple, Octameron Associates, Alexandria, VA.

*English Language and Orientation Programs in the United State*s, James E. Driscoll, Institute for International Education, Washington, DC.

Get Organized!, Edward B. Fiske and Phyllis Steinbrecher, Peterson's Guides, Princeton, NJ.

Getting In!, Paulo De Oliviera and Steve Cohen, Workman Publishing, New York, NY.

Going the Distance, Stephen Figler and Howard Figler, Peterson's Guides, Princeton, NJ.

Guide to American Art Schools, John D. Werenko, Penguin Books, New York, NY.

Guide to Architecture Schools in North America, Association of Collegiate Schools of Architecture Press.

Guide to Catholic Colleges and Universities The College Connection, Flushing, New York.

Handbook for College Admissions: A Family Guide, Thomas C. Hayden, Peterson's Guides, Princeton, NJ.

How the Military Will Help You Pay for College, Don M. Betteron, Peterson's Guides, Princeton, NJ.

How to Get Into the Right College, Edward B. Fiske, Times Books, New York, NY.

How to Get into US. Service Academies, William Bennett Cassidy, Arco Publishing, New York, NY.

How To Prepare For The ACT, Barron's Educational Series, Happauge, NY.

Index of Majors, College Board, New York, NY.

Introducing. the New SAT: The College Board's Official Guide, College Board, New York, NY.

Jewish Life On Campus, B'nai B'rith Hillel Foundations, Washington, DC.

Letting Go: A Parents' Guide to Today's College Experience, Karen Levin Coburn and Madge Lawrence Treeger, Adler and PBET.

Looking Beyond the Ivy League: Finding The College That's Right For You, Loren Pope, Viking Penguin, New York, NY.

Lovejoy's College Guide for the Learning Disabled, Charles T. Straughn, Monarch Press, New York, NY.

Lovejoy's College Guide, Lovejoy's Educational Guides, Monarch Press, New York, NY.

Major Decisions: A Guide to College Majors, Richard A. Blumenthal and Joseph A. Despres, Orchard House, Concord, MA.

*National Directory of College Athlete*s (Men's and Women's Editions), NCAA, Collegiate Directories, Cleveland, OH.

Official Guide to the ACT Assessment, Harcourt, Brace, Jovanovich Publishers, New York, NY.

On Writing the College Application, Harold Bauld, Barnes and Noble Books, New York, NY.

Parenting Through the College Years, Norman Giddan and Sally Vallongo, Williamson Publishing, Charlotte, VT.

Peterson's Competitive Colleges, Peterson's Guides, Princeton, NJ.

Peterson's Drug and Alcohol Programs and Policies at Four-Year Colleges, Janet Schneider and Bunny Porter-Shirley, Peterson's Guides, Princeton, NJ .

Peterson's Guide to Colleges with Programs for Learning Disabled Student', Charles T. Mangrum and Steven S. Strichart, Peterson's Guides, Princeton, NJ.

Peterson's Guide To Four-Year Colleges, Peterson's Guides, Princeton, NJ.

Peterson's National College Databank, Peterson's Guides, Princeton, NJ.

Playing the Selective College Admissions Game, Richard Moll, Penguin Books, New York, NY.

Putting Your Kids Through College, Scott Edelstein, Consumer Reports Books, Consumers Union, Mount Vernon, NY.

Qualifying for Admission to the Service Academies, A Student's Guide, Robert F. Collins, Rosen Publishing Group, New York, NY.

Reserve Officer Training Corps: Campus Paths to Service Commissions, Robert F. Collins, Rosen Publishing Group, New York, NY.

ROTC College Handbook, Arco Publishing, New York, NY.

Rueg's Recommendations on the Colleges, Frederick E. Rur, Rugg's Recommendations, Sarasota, FL.

Scaling the Ivy Wall: 12 Winning Steps to College Admission, Howard Greene and Robert Minton, Little, Brown and Company, Boston, MA.

Scholarships for International Students, Anna Leider, Octameron Associates, Alexandria, VA.

Test Skills: A Test Preparation Program for the PSAT/NMS, College Board, New York, NY.

The Admissions Essay, Helen W. Power and Robert DiAntonio, Lyle Stuart, Secaucus, NJ.

The Black Student's Guide to Colleges, Barry Beckham, Beckham House Publishers, Providence, RI.

The College Entrance Predictor, Clifford J. Caine, Stephen Greene Press, Lexington, MA.

The College Finder: 475 Ways to Find the Right School for You, Steven Antonoff, Ballantine Books, New York, N.Y.

The College Handbook Foreign Student Supplement, College Board, New York, NY.

The College Guide for Parents, Charles J. Shields, College Board, New York, NY.

The Complete Guide to College Visits, Janet Spencer and Sandra Maleson, Citadel Press, New York, NY.

The Complete Handbook for College Women, Carol Weinberg, New York University Press, New York, NY.

The Directory of Athletic Scholarships, Alan Green, Facts on File Publications, New York, NY.

The Engineering Career Guide, William F. Shanahan, Arco Publishing, New York, NY.

The FCLD Learning Disabilities Resource Guide, Foundation for Children with Learning · Disabilities, New York, NY.

The Fisher-Guide to Colleges, Edward B. Fiske, Times'Books, New York, NY.

The Gay, Lesbian and Bisexual Students' Guide to Colleges, Universities and Graduate Schools, Jan Mitchell-Sherrill and Craig Hardesty, New York University Press, New York, NY.

The GIS Guide to Four-Year Colleges, Guidance Information System, Houghton Mifflin Company, Boston, MA.

The Insider's Guide To The College, Staff of the Yale Daily News, St. Martin's Press, New York, NY.

The Jewish Student's Guide, American Colleges Lee and Lana Goldberg, Shapolsky Publishers, New York, NY.

The K & W Guide to Colleges for the Learning Disabled, Marybeth Kravets and Amy Wax, Harper Collins, New York, NY.

The Multicultural Student's Guide to Colleges, Robert Mitchell.

The Official Guide to SAT-II: Subject Tests, College Board, New York, NY.

The One-Hour College Applicant, Lois Rochester and Judy Mandell, Mustang Publishing, New Haven, CT.

The Performing Arts Major's College Guide, Carole J. Everett, Arco, Prentice Hall, New York, NY.

The Public Ivy, Richard Moll, Viking Penguin, New York, NY.

The Right College, College Research Group of Concord, MA, Arco Publishing, New York, NY.

The Student Guide to Catholic Colleges and Universities, John R. Crocker, Harper and Row Publishers, New York, NY.

The Winning Edge: A Complete Guide to Intercollegiate Athletic Programs, Frances and James Killpatrick, Octameron Associates, Alexandria, VA.

Unlocking Potential: College and Other Choices for Learning Disabled People—A Step-by-Step Guide, Barbara Schreiber and Jeanne I Alpers, Adler and Adler Publishers, Bethesda, MD.

Who Gets In? A Guide to College Selection, Dan Tyson, Graphic Publishing, Wichita, KS.

Write Your Way into College, George Ehrenhaft, Barron's Educational Series, Happauge, NY.

Writing Your College Application Essay, Sarah Myers McGinty, College Board, New York, NY.

Financial Aid References

Barron's Dollars For Scholars: Barron's Complete College Financing Guide, Marguerite J. Dennis, Barron's Educational Series, Happauge, NY.

Blum's Guides to College Money Series, including Free Money for Humanities and Social Sciences, Free money for Mathematics and Natural Sciences, and Free Money for Professional Studies, Laurie Blum, Paragon House Publishers, New York, NY.

College Check Mate, Financial Aid , Octameron Associates, Alexandria, VA.

College Costs and Financial Aid Handbook, The College Board, Princeton, NJ.

College Financial Aid Annual, College Research Group of Concord, MA, Arco Publishing, New York, NY.

Cutting College Costs, James P. Duffy, Barnes and Noble Publishers, New York, NY.

Directory of Financial Aids for Minorities 1991-1993, Gail Ann Schlachler.

Don't Miss Out The A's and B's of Academic Scholarships College Grants, Octameron Associates, Alexandria, VA.

Earn & Learn: Cooperative Education Opportunities Offered by the Federal Government, Joseph M. Re.

Financial Aid Financer! Expert Answers to College Financing Questions, Octameron Associates, Alexandria, VA.

Financial Aid for Higher Education Orion Keeslar, William C. Brown Publishers, Dubuque, IA.

Financial Aid Officers: What They Do To You—And For You, Donald Moore.

Financing A College Education: The Essential Guide for the 90s, Judith B. Margolin, Plenum Press.

Loans and Grants from Uncle Sam: Am I Eligible and For How Much,? Octameron Associates, Alexandria, VA.

Lovejoy's Guide to Financial Aid, Robert and Anna Leider, Monarch Press, New York, NY.

195

Need A Lift?, American Legion Educational Program, Indianapolis, IN.

Paying Less for College 1994, The Complete Guide to $28 Billion in Financial Aid.

Peterson's College Money Handbook, Peterson's Guides. Princeton, NJ.

Peterson's College Money Handbook, Peterson's Guides, Princeton, NJ.

The A's and B's of Academic Scholarships, Daphne A. Philos.

The Black Student's Guide to Scholarships, Ernestine Whiting, ed., Beckham House Publishers, Silver Spring, MD.

The College Blue Book, 24th Edition, Scholarships, Fellowships, Grants and Loans.

The College Cost Book, College Board, New York, NY.

The Scholarship Book: The Complete Guide to Private-Sector Scholarships, Grants, and Loans For Undergraduates, Daniel J. Cassidy and Michael J. Alves, Prentice Hall Publishers, Englewood Cliffs, NJ.

The Student Guide, Financial Aid From the U.S. Department of Education, 1995-96.

They Do To You and For You, Octameron Associates, Alexandria, VA.

Winning Money For College: The High School Student's Guide to Scholarship Contests, Alan Deutschman, Peterson's Guides, Princeton, NJ.

Major Websites for College Admissions

www.collegeview.com

www.collegeboard.org/gp/hartman/html/intro.html

www.collegenet.com

www.usnews.com

www.collegeboard.org

www.princetonreview.com

www.petersons.com/ugrad/

www.ed.gov/

www.fastweb.com

www.fafsa.ed.gov

www.finaid.org

www.collegeedge.com

www.kaplan.com

http://collegeapps.miningco.com/education/collegeapps/

http://www.bignerds.com/ce/ce.shtml

http://www.collegexpress.com/

http://www.myessay.com/

http://www.collegenet.com/

http://www.edonline.com/collegecompass/

http://www.sourcepath.com/

http://www.collegeprepservices.com/home.html

http://www.college-scholarships.com/100college.htm

http://www.reverse-lookup.com/collegest.htm

http://www.nacac.com/index.html

http://embark.lycos.com/

http://www.jayi.com/

http://www.tsoft.com/~bdoolin/bethany/college_aid.html

http://collegecountdownkit.com/sitecont.htm

http://www.wcco.com/education/fouryear/

http://www.collegequest.com/plugin.nd/CollegeQuest/pgGateway

http://www.collegebound.net/

http://www.commonapp.org/

http://www.collegekey.com/

http://www.collegenight.com/

http://learninfreedom.org/colleges_4_hmsc.html

http://www.collegesource.org/home.asp

http://www.e-hound.org/

http://www.ecollegebid.org/

http://www.edcasworldwide.com/

http://www.stanford.edu/~jerfox/laissez-faire-1999-2000.txt

http://www.gocollege.com/

Index

B

C

D

E

F

G

H

I

J

T

Printed in the United States
1004000003B